● = COACHING THROUGH EFFECTIVE FEEDBACK

A Practical Guide To
Successful Communication

Paul J. Jerome

Jossey-Bass
Pfeiffer
San Francisco

RICHARD
CHANG
ASSOCIATES

Published by

350 Sansome Street, 5th Floor
San Francisco, California 94104-1342
(415) 433-1740; Fax (415) 433-0499
(800) 274-4434; Fax (800) 569-0443

Visit our website at: www.pfeiffer.com

Printing   10   9   8   7   6   5   4   3   2

ACKNOWLEDGMENTS

About The Author

Paul J. Jerome is Vice President of Richard Chang Associates, Inc., a diversified organizational improvement consulting firm based in Irvine, California. He is an experienced management consultant and business executive specializing in executive development, management training, team building, and performance management. Paul is widely recognized for his creative design and enthusiastic delivery of practical management tools and techniques.

Paul would like to acknowledge the support of the entire team of professionals at Richard Chang Associates, Inc. for their contribution to the guidebook development process. In addition, special thanks are extended to the many client organizations who have helped shape the practical ideas and proven methods shared in this guidebook.

Additional Credits

Editor:	Sarah Ortlieb Fraser
Reviewers:	Ruth Larsen and Jim Greeley
Layout:	Christina Slater
Cover Design:	John Odam Design Associates

PREFACE

The 1990's have already presented individuals and organizations with some very difficult challenges to face and overcome. So who will have the advantage as we move toward the year 2000 and beyond?

The advantage will belong to those with a commitment to continuous learning. Whether on an individual basis or as an entire organization, one key ingredient to building a continuous learning environment is *The Practical Guidebook Collection* brought to you by the Publications Division of Richard Chang Associates, Inc.

After understanding the future *"learning needs"* expressed by our clients and other potential customers, we are pleased to publish *The Practical Guidebook Collection*. These guidebooks are designed to provide you with proven, *"real-world"* tips, tools, and techniques—on a wide range of subjects—that you can apply in the workplace and/or on a personal level immediately.

Once you've had a chance to benefit from *The Practical Guidebook Collection*, please share your feedback with us. We've included a brief *Evaluation and Feedback Form* at the end of the guidebook that you can fax to us at (949) 727-7007.

With your feedback, we can continuously improve the resources we are providing through the Publications Division of Richard Chang Associates, Inc.

Wishing you successful reading,

Richard Y. Chang
President and CEO
Richard Chang Associates, Inc.

TABLE OF CONTENTS

"Over 60 percent of all management problems result from faulty communications."

Peter Drucker

"If an organization is to work effectively, the communication should be through the most effective channel regardless of the organization chart."

David Packard, founder, Hewlett-Packard

"It takes an average person almost twice as long to understand a sentence that uses a negative approach than it does to understand a positive sentence."

John H. Reitmann, psychiatrist

"If you have nothing nice to say, don't say it."

Mom

INTRODUCTION

Giving and receiving performance feedback successfully is one of the most critical and difficult, yet often undeveloped and undervalued interpersonal skills in the modern workplace. Regardless of how complex and sophisticated the *"high-tech"* business world becomes, people will still need to communicate comfortably and effectively with other people.

A solid foundation of coaching skills, particularly in the area of giving and receiving feedback, is a must for individuals at all levels in organizations, especially as the constant need for organizational change continues to reshape the way we interact at work.

Why Read This Guidebook?

This guidebook gives you the tool you need to prepare and provide meaningful feedback. Feedback involves praising others to reinforce their outstanding performance and criticizing others to improve work situations.

The tool—called the Feedback Planner—works every time, whether you're dealing with an employee who reports to you, a coworker, or a boss.

Who Should Read This Guidebook?

Supervisors, managers, self-directed team members and leaders will gain a valuable tool from this guidebook.

Professionals in the fields of human resources, training, organizational development, and total quality management can also use this critical coaching formula.

Indeed, the Feedback Planner can help anyone looking to enhance key interpersonal skills, improve individual and team performance, and promote continuous improvement.

When And How To Use It

Use the Feedback Planner whenever you need to criticize or praise someone. Don't just use it at work. You can also use this process to improve behaviors and situations involving your family, friends, or acquaintances.

You'll find many examples of completed Feedback Planners in this guidebook. Although the Planner provides an effective formula for giving praise to reinforce desirable behavior, other examples here illustrate ways to give criticism. This is because giving criticism tends to be the most difficult challenge for many people—and for good reason. Careless criticism risks relationships and morale. The Feedback Planner neutralizes problems by laying a foundation for action instead of blame.

Please reproduce the Feedback Planner form in Appendix B and use it to collect, examine, and share your thoughts about situations you want to improve.

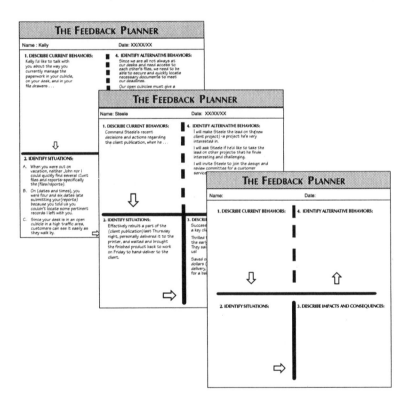

Note: It is not the intent of this author to characterize certain personality traits as being gender specific.

CHAPTER TWO

NEEDING A FEEDBACK PLANNER

Giving Feedback Is Part Of Coaching

Effective coaching is akin to successful management—both can produce winning teams. In business, coaching is the ongoing process of guiding and developing employees.

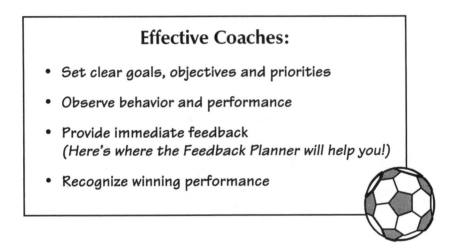

Effective Coaches:

- Set clear goals, objectives and priorities

- Observe behavior and performance

- Provide immediate feedback
  (Here's where the Feedback Planner will help you!)

- Recognize winning performance

This guidebook focuses on an effective model for providing immediate feedback—the Feedback Planner.

In order to provide effective feedback, it is important to first understand the four stages of the feedback process.

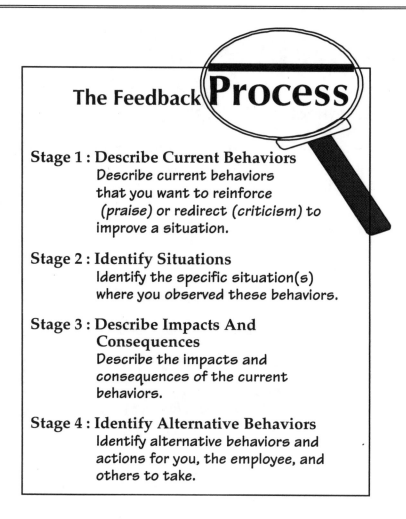

The Feedback **Process**

Stage 1 : Describe Current Behaviors
Describe current behaviors
that you want to reinforce
(praise) or redirect (criticism) to
improve a situation.

Stage 2 : Identify Situations
Identify the specific situation(s)
where you observed these behaviors.

Stage 3 : Describe Impacts And
Consequences
Describe the impacts and
consequences of the current
behaviors.

Stage 4 : Identify Alternative Behaviors
Identify alternative behaviors and
actions for you, the employee, and
others to take.

"Disruptive Behaviors" Sabotage Feedback Efforts

Sharing feedback, especially criticism, is difficult enough as it is for most of us. Yet, it can become more agonizing if we become part of the problem. Wrongful criticism is dangerous. It can eat up energy and erode people's spirits.

False or generalized praise also misses the mark. No, the risks are not as high if we mess up a compliment (versus a criticism). But the potential gains are lost.

The Feedback Planner helps you avoid giving ineffective feedback *(with "disruptive behaviors")*.

The Feedback Planner is based on a foundation of strategies necessary to enhance the effectiveness of your communication while avoiding typical disruptive behaviors. You will find the disruptive behaviors grouped under each of the four stages of the feedback process.

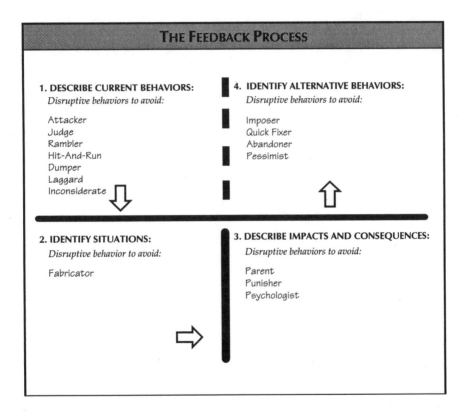

THE FEEDBACK PROCESS

1. DESCRIBE CURRENT BEHAVIORS:
Disruptive behaviors to avoid:

Attacker
Judge
Rambler
Hit-And-Run
Dumper
Laggard
Inconsiderate

4. IDENTIFY ALTERNATIVE BEHAVIORS:
Disruptive behaviors to avoid:

Imposer
Quick Fixer
Abandoner
Pessimist

2. IDENTIFY SITUATIONS:
Disruptive behavior to avoid:

Fabricator

3. DESCRIBE IMPACTS AND CONSEQUENCES:
Disruptive behaviors to avoid:

Parent
Punisher
Psychologist

Scenarios of disruptive behaviors will introduce and demonstrate the need for the Feedback Planner strategies.

These strategies will help you *"paint a clearer picture"* for the receiver of your feedback!

Chapter Eight will show you precisely how to use these strategies.

Stage 1: Describe Current Behaviors

The Attacker

We've all seen intimidation at work. Intimidation means to frighten, to inhibit, or to discourage as if by threat. It's a coward's way to change behavior.

Attackers challenge personal traits instead of specific behaviors. They gain support by threatening—in a spoken or unspoken manner—to hurt or embarrass. They knowingly or unknowingly go for the jugular vein by saying:

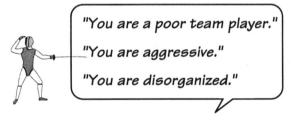

"You are a poor team player."

"You are aggressive."

"You are disorganized."

The result is often a predictable defense, *"No, I'm not."* A shutdown of communication follows.

The Attacker launches into . . .

a personal attack. *"Scott, your office is a mess. It's a wonder how you find anything under all of these scattered papers. Get organized, will ya?"*

Scott reacts from a whole different perspective. *"What's the problem? I just run my show differently, but I know where everything is. Now you're telling me I'm disorganized? I can't believe this."*

The Attacker should back off and:

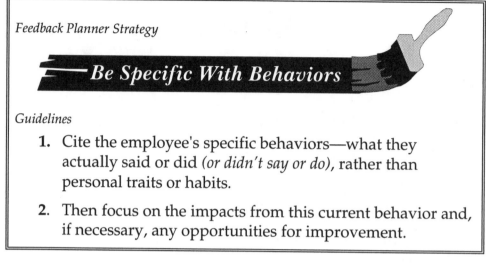

Feedback Planner Strategy

Be Specific With Behaviors

Guidelines

1. Cite the employee's specific behaviors—what they actually said or did *(or didn't say or do)*, rather than personal traits or habits.

2. Then focus on the impacts from this current behavior and, if necessary, any opportunities for improvement.

The Judge

The Judge does not understand the concept of *"shades of gray."* Everything in his world fits into a narrow classification. She's right or wrong. He's good or bad. The Judge derives these assessments without benefit of facts or concrete information. He distorts reality and sells his people short with comments such as:

"You did a poor job."

"That was a bad call."

"Good work."

Professionals know when they're meeting, exceeding, or falling short of expectations. If they don't, that's what they need to have *described* to them—not a general evaluation of being *"good or bad."* Loaded, subjective opinions and careless classifications breed distance among people. Judges can leave the wrong impression *(usually a misunderstanding)*, and miss the point—to reinforce or redirect behavior to improve a situation.

Even if the judgment is positive praise *("Good job")*, it often reminds the receiver of a past authoritarian figure—a family member or a third grade English teacher saying, *"Nice job, Billy!"*

The Judge was on a recess . . .

while Laurie worked for two months on a new computer program to meet the growing needs of the Expediting Department. It was a complex assignment that required a thorough needs analysis and integrated design of a user-friendly software system. She's received accolades from Expediting, yet little recognition from her boss, the Judge.

When she reminded the Judge of her accomplishments in a staff meeting, the Judge responded, *"Oh, yes. I hear you did really good work. Nice job. Let's hear it for Laurie!"*

Laurie followed with a smile of thanks, yet thought, *"You have no idea what I did and why my work was successful. I know I did a nice job. I wanted to hear more—maybe how my performance will pay off in the future? Well, I guess it's better than being overlooked or chewed out."*

Two weeks later, in a private meeting, the Judge refers to a task that Laurie has not completed yet. *"You've done a bad job of getting your time allocation records in."*

Laurie clams up, thinking, *"So much for that last success in Expediting."*

The Judge should lose the gavel and:

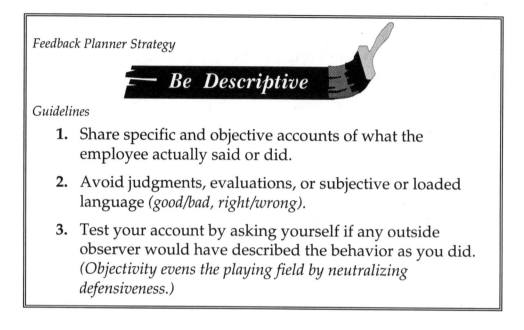

Feedback Planner Strategy

Be Descriptive

Guidelines

1. Share specific and objective accounts of what the employee actually said or did.

2. Avoid judgments, evaluations, or subjective or loaded language *(good/bad, right/wrong).*

3. Test your account by asking yourself if any outside observer would have described the behavior as you did. *(Objectivity evens the playing field by neutralizing defensiveness.)*

The Rambler

The Rambler delivers long-winded lectures, and does not seek input or responses. He knows the score and, as soon as he's concluded his lecture, he thinks his employee does, too. The Rambler relies on power and often says things like:

BLAH, BLAH,   *BLAH, BLAH*

"Do you know why it didn't work? I'll tell you why."

"Pay attention. I'm going to explain to you exactly what you did and what I expect in the future."

BLAH,   *BLAH*

"Hey, don't worry about it. Let me tell you what I did when I was in your position . . . "

Somewhere along the road, the receiver forgets where they were going. The Rambler's blithering has overshadowed his message.

The Rambler overwhelms . . .

Virginia with a reprimand for not being around the office when he needed her yesterday. The Rambler starts in, *"I don't know what's going on in your personal life, but it's affecting your attitude. You're never in the office when I need you. When I was up and coming, I was available 24 hours a day. My boss could get me whenever she needed me. In fact, when I transferred to this department, no let's see, it was Operations, five, no ten years ago . . . "*

A half-hour later, Virginia is still slumped in her chair listening to the Rambler. She hasn't yet uttered one word of defense.

Virginia is thinking, *"What did I do to deserve this? When I'm out of the office, I'm in the field with clients. I tell our receptionist where I am. And, what's wrong with my attitude? If he shuts up for a minute, I can give my side of the story and get back to work."*

The Rambler should rein in his lips and:

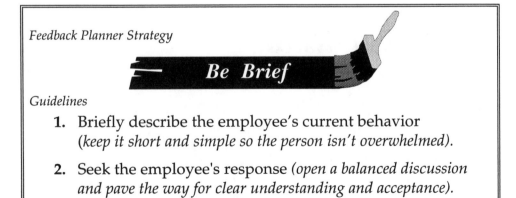

Feedback Planner Strategy

Be Brief

Guidelines

1. Briefly describe the employee's current behavior *(keep it short and simple so the person isn't overwhelmed)*.

2. Seek the employee's response *(open a balanced discussion and pave the way for clear understanding and acceptance)*.

The Hit-And-Run

The Hit-And-Run makes a quick and vague point and disappears. She often uses a voice mail, E-mail, memo, freeway-speed-pass-by in the hallway, or some other one-way communication process. And she's usually not available for questions and answers. People are left wondering where they stand—other than in the dark:

> *"Actually, I'd prefer if you'd do it differently. Thanks!"*
>
> *"Don't worry about it. There's always room for improvement."*
>
> *"Please fix that next time, will ya?"*

Why does the Hit-And-Run do it? Is she too busy, afraid of confrontation, shy, insensitive, preoccupied, or *"genetically vague"*? Desirable feedback, whether praise or criticism, can be misconstrued.

The Hit-And-Run wrecks . . .

Donald's day with a voice mail: *"Donald, to shorten your future meetings and to free yourself up, you can distribute background reading materials in advance. Talk to you soon!"*

Donald is wondering, *"Hum. That was strange. A nice suggestion out of the blue? I need to thank her. But, wait—there was no 'hello.' Was I just criticized? Are my meetings unproductive? Wait a minute! Maybe she was complimenting me. Yes, she likes my work and wants me freed up from my unproductive meetings! But why did she send the message last night? My last meeting was two weeks ago and my next meeting isn't until next—uh oh. When are we going to talk? I don't have time to put these materials together by next week!"*

The Hit-And-Run should apply the brakes and:

Feedback Planner Strategy

Be Available and Open

Guidelines

1. Be available to share and discuss your observations, comments, and suggestions with others.

2. Solicit all sides of the story to get a complete picture.

3. Actively listen to employees and then paraphrase what you believe was said to make sure everyone understands the situation.

The Dumper

The Dumper unloads on people. He doesn't put criticisms into context—he just lists. He stores them in gunny sacks and then dumps them *all* on your head:

"Please take notes. We've got a lot to discuss and time is short."

"Oh, while we're at it—one more thing . . . "

"There's a number of things I want to cover with you."

Stand back. Take cover. You're being bombed. If the Dumper is also loud and aggressive, you'll feel chewed up and then spat out.

What's sad is that the Dumper may have a valid point worth discussing. It just gets lost in the shuffle as the small hairs rise on the receiver's neck, along with the length of their defense—which they'll get to when and if they can get a chance.

The Dumper unloads . . .

on Jean after she missed a deadline. Not only does he ridicule her in public, he piles on every other negative assessment he's ever had about Jean: *"You can't deliver on time. You're always taking the easy way out. You haven't even started the big sales report, and you're late a lot."*

Jean's thinking, *"Yes, the sales report is under a stack of papers on my desk, but it's not due for a—wait a minute—what has my sales report got to do with a deadline missed when I was sick yesterday? And, what's this 'late' business?"*

The Dumper should lighten up and:

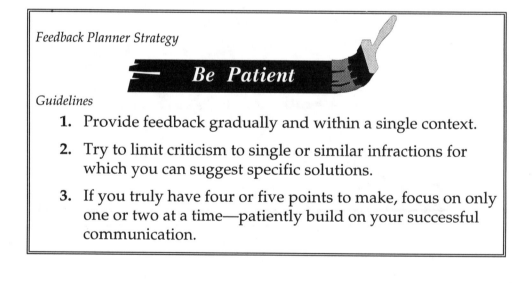

Feedback Planner Strategy

Be Patient

Guidelines

1. Provide feedback gradually and within a single context.

2. Try to limit criticism to single or similar infractions for which you can suggest specific solutions.

3. If you truly have four or five points to make, focus on only one or two at a time—patiently build on your successful communication.

The Laggard

The Laggard dilly-dallies. He delivers criticism, or praise for that matter, whenever the spirit moves him, if he remembers:

"Oh, by the way . . . "

"Now that you mentioned it—no, I wasn't happy with that job."

"Yes. I'm glad you brought that up. I've been meaning to talk with you."

With time goes memory. With memory goes the accuracy of facts, and the effectiveness of praise or criticism.

Delayed praise can be grossly misinterpreted: *"Is she just trying to be nice, or did she mean it?" "If he was that thrilled, he would have said so earlier."* Delayed criticism is equally risky: *"What's bugging him?" "I can't believe she waited until now to tell me this—I could have corrected this mistake a month ago!"*

The Laggard was unmoved . . .

as Duane finished the video for the new client two days ahead of schedule. The client praised it as the most effective piece of work she'd ever seen and ordered a second series.

Three weeks pass before the Laggard sees Duane in the hall. He asks Duane where he's been, and remembers the video project. The Laggard says, *"Hey. Nice work on that auto parts video, Duane."*

Duane responds, *"I didn't do an auto parts video. I did the customer relations series."*

The Laggard doesn't miss a beat, *"That's what I meant. Good job. Keep up the good work."*

Duane's thinking, *"I really thought that video was great. I put my best effort forth. It must not have been that impressive if the Laggard doesn't even remember what I did. What if I never ran into him in the hallway? I would have heard nothing at all. Jerk!"*

The Laggard should wake up and:

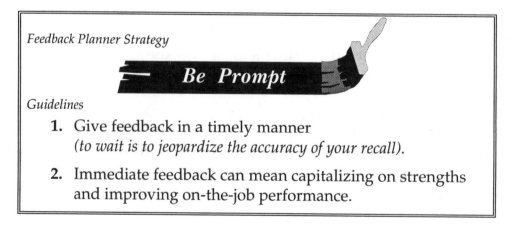

Feedback Planner Strategy

Be Prompt

Guidelines

1. Give feedback in a timely manner
   (to wait is to jeopardize the accuracy of your recall).

2. Immediate feedback can mean capitalizing on strengths and improving on-the-job performance.

The Inconsiderate

The Inconsiderate gives no thought to the time and place they choose to deliver feedback. The Inconsiderate's style can be perceived as insensitive and thoughtless:

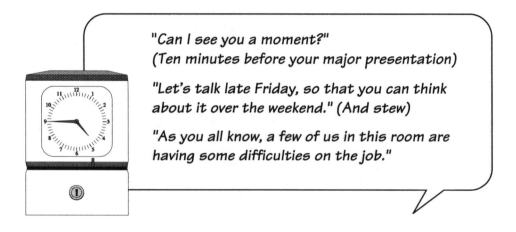

"Can I see you a moment?"
(Ten minutes before your major presentation)

"Let's talk late Friday, so that you can think about it over the weekend." (And stew)

"As you all know, a few of us in this room are having some difficulties on the job."

There is no right or wrong time or place to give and receive feedback, but there are more and less desirable times and places. For example, praising in public can be a real ego-booster to some and an embarrassment to others. Criticizing someone at the end of the day can seem considerate *(e.g., you didn't want to ruin their day, you wanted to give them time to think about it overnight)*, or spineless *(e.g., you didn't want to talk, so you dumped it and ran)*. See Chapter Nine for more insight.

The Inconsiderate barges into . . .

the crowded newsroom and vents to the staff, *"This copy's got two typos and a misspelled name in it. What are we paying for here? If we can't do better than this, some of us will find our names on the obit desk. Got it?"*

Everyone in the room knew he was talking about Karl and Alice's work. The two were mortified. A colleague says to Karl, *"I can't believe he screamed at all of us for something like that. What did I do?"*

Karl responds defensively, *"Hey! What about us? We double-checked everything in the story. Imagine how we feel being humiliated in front of everybody!"*

The Inconsiderate should get in touch and:

Feedback Planner Strategy

⇐ Be Sensitive To Time and Place

Guidelines

1. Present feedback at an appropriate time and setting. *(Even the most thoughtful feedback shared at the wrong time can do more harm than good!)*

2. When in doubt, ask the employee when and where he would like to talk.

3. Share criticism and praise only with the people they involve.

CHAPTER THREE WORKSHEET:
APPLYING STRATEGIES TO AVOID
UNSUCCESSFUL EXPERIENCES

Answer the following questions and apply the key learning points from Chapter Three.

1. Describe one of your more *unsuccessful experiences* giving and/or receiving feedback. What was specifically said or done and by whom? What were the results?

_____

_____

_____

_____

2. Identify one to two *disruptive behaviors* that were a part of these experiences *(e.g., Attacker, Judge, etc.)*.

_____

_____

_____

3. Select one or two Feedback Planner Strategies that will help guide you in the right direction should you have a similar experience *(e.g., be specific with behaviors, be descriptive, etc.)*.

_____

_____

_____

CHAPTER FOUR

STAGE 2 : IDENTIFY SITUATIONS

The Fabricator

The Fabricator needs frequent reality checks. He lives in a world devoid of fact. He uses unfounded or overblown assessments to gauge employee behaviors:

> *"I've told you fifty times to . . . "*
>
> *"Either you didn't know what to do, or you made the wrong choice."*
>
> *"You always do that, and you know it!"*

The Fabricator doesn't want to waste time researching facts and figures—why confuse things with details? He knows what he's going to find. And since documentation can be interpreted in so many ways, the Fabricator feels he's really doing the employee a favor by not dealing with it at all!

The Fabricator also won't check for others' observations and perceptions—why ask for more opinions when you already have one? He heard what he needed to hear from the old reliable grapevine. The lunchroom is a gold mine for this kind of stuff. That's enough—talking to others more will only stir up the pot and embarrass the employee. And besides, what do these people know that the Fabricator doesn't?

What about checking further with the employee? Maybe the Fabricator doesn't have a complete picture. Who are you kidding? Here's where the true talent of the Fabricator shines through. You see, it's an art form to creatively fill in the blanks without all of the puzzle pieces! And the missing pieces are irrelevant in the eyes of the Fabricator. All he really wants is the attention of the receiver and a change of behavior now, and he'll do whatever it takes to get there. *"Never say never,"* was never said by the Fabricator. *"If it works, use it!"* is his motto.

The Fabricator doesn't even collect his thoughts. He's confident that his exaggerations and embellishments, coupled with a loud voice and enlarged jugular vein, will do the trick! And he gets away with it time and time again. But there are a number of flaws in his approach.

This behavior usually provokes an easy and sound defense. All the receiver has to do is come up with one exception and all of the wind is taken out of the sail. For example: *"You're always late."* *"I wasn't late today."* End of conversation.

The Fabricator magnifies . . .

Larry's efforts in creating a minor four-color graphic to accompany a marketing brochure: *"You always get too bogged down in the details and never see the big picture. This graphic is nice but not worth all that time."*

Larry responds quickly, *"I put in as much time as was necessary to get it right—most of it was on my own time. It's an important document. And what 'big picture' am I missing?"*

"This one—you always spend too much time on these things," the Fabricator explained. *(Of course, he didn't say how much time is "too much.")*

Larry continues under his breath: *"This is the thanks I get? I've learned my lesson. We want below average work around here."*

The Fabricator should toss the *"big fish"* stories and:

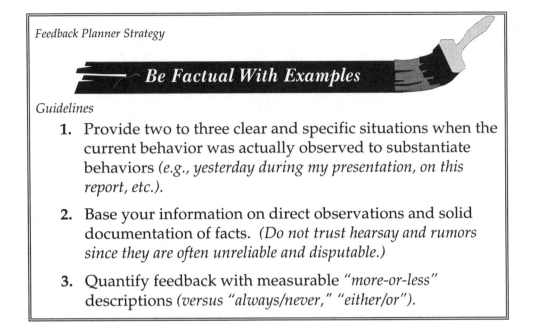

Feedback Planner Strategy

Be Factual With Examples

Guidelines

1. Provide two to three clear and specific situations when the current behavior was actually observed to substantiate behaviors *(e.g., yesterday during my presentation, on this report, etc.)*.

2. Base your information on direct observations and solid documentation of facts. *(Do not trust hearsay and rumors since they are often unreliable and disputable.)*

3. Quantify feedback with measurable *"more-or-less"* descriptions *(versus "always/never," "either/or").*

Stage 3: Describe Impacts And Consequences

The Parent

The Parent often relies on personal likes and dislikes when choosing behaviors to criticize or praise. He wants others to be like him. If necessary and possible, the Parent will send people off on *"guilt trips"* or will pull rank to get his way:

> "It's just not the kind of behavior I want around here."
>
> "I expected much more from you, and you disappointed me."
>
> "Why are you fighting me on this? I just want what's best for you."

People resent being told to be like others, just because they're different. If there's no reason to change their current behaviors *(i.e., if there are no negative impacts or consequences)*, then the Parent should accept them.

The Parent belittles . . .

Chris' potential. Chris is seen by his coworkers as bright and creative. They feel he's the most qualified for the promotional opportunity.

Yet, the Parent presents a different view to the Big Boss on why he turned down Chris' promotion. *"It doesn't have anything to do with the fact that he's gay. He's just got too much flair. Our clients are too conservative to appreciate Chris. It's best for all of us, including Chris, if he's kept behind the scenes."*

Chris found out about the Parent's views through the grapevine. He thinks, *"What did I do wrong? I've been producing twice as much as everyone else. Clients love my work. My coworkers respect my expertise and leadership. I just don't get it."*

The Parent should remove the curfew and:

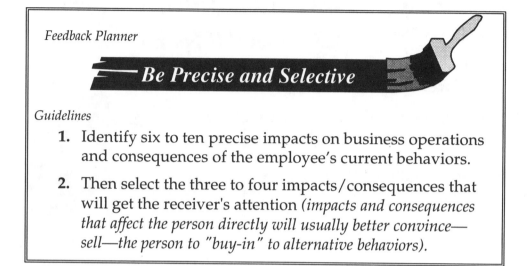

Feedback Planner

Be Precise and Selective

Guidelines

1. Identify six to ten precise impacts on business operations and consequences of the employee's current behaviors.

2. Then select the three to four impacts/consequences that will get the receiver's attention (*impacts and consequences that affect the person directly will usually better convince— sell—the person to "buy-in" to alternative behaviors*).

The Punisher

The Punisher focuses only on the downside. He tries to change behavior by solely dwelling on the extreme negative impacts and punitive consequences of current behavior to scare a person straight:

"This will get you fired. It's your choice."

"I don't know why you continue to do this. Nothing good ever comes from it."

"Don't come running to me when it blows up. You caused it."

Granted, some behaviors *do* have devastating impacts and severe consequences (*e.g., driving a company vehicle while under the influence of alcohol or drugs, fighting, stealing, etc.*). But most of the time, we're not dealing with this type of situation. There's less reason to play *"the heavy"* to make a good point for an alternative behavior.

The Punisher tears into . . .

a coworker, Carol. "If we would have just used the software program we had, we would have been done already. But no, you had to install something new. Now you've done it. We're behind schedule and the Big Boss is going to fry us when we miss the delivery date to the customer!"

Carol defends herself. "Relax. This new software will save us hundreds of hours on the back end of the project. It was worth the slight delay. We'll exceed the delivery date. And I got the Big Boss' support."

"He doesn't know what he's doing either! Don't come running to me when the customer comes looking for heads to roll," snaps the Punisher.

The Punisher should look for a few silver linings and:

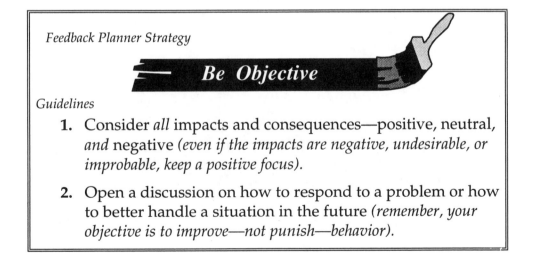

Feedback Planner Strategy

Be Objective

Guidelines

1. Consider *all* impacts and consequences—positive, neutral, *and* negative (*even if the impacts are negative, undesirable, or improbable, keep a positive focus*).

2. Open a discussion on how to respond to a problem or how to better handle a situation in the future (*remember, your objective is to improve—not punish—behavior*).

The Psychologist

The Psychologist rejects factual cause-and-effect behaviors in favor of probing employees' psychological motivations. In essence, Psychologists like to play with people's heads:

"You knew what you were doing. Now live with the consequences."

"You must have wanted to hurt me, or you wouldn't have said that."

"I know why you acted that way. It's because . . . "

The Psychologist obsesses with *"why"* to seek deep underlying motives and intentions. It's often a fruitless quest because deep motives may not exist or be very difficult to get. More often the *"why's"* of a situation are not as important as figuring out how to change it.

The Psychologist leans back in his chair . . .

as Sally explains that she didn't mean to go over his head to get an assignment changed. In an impromptu meeting, she suggested the change to the Big Boss, and the Big Boss liked it.

The Psychologist tells Sally that she made a big mistake going outside the chain of command, and that he knows why: *"You knew very well what you were doing. You did it to make a name for yourself and make me look bad."*

Sally replies defensively, *"No. That's not why I did it. The opportunity just presented itself. I thought you'd be thrilled to get this project off our backs. Aren't we on the same team?"*

The Psychologist delves deeper. *"Don't change the subject. If you didn't want to overstep your boundaries, you wouldn't have. I'm tired of your negative reactions every time you get an assignment you don't like. You're a prima donna, Sally. You were probably a spoiled kid who learned how to get your way by making a scene."*

Sally walks off in a blue funk.

The Psychologist should stop analyzing and:

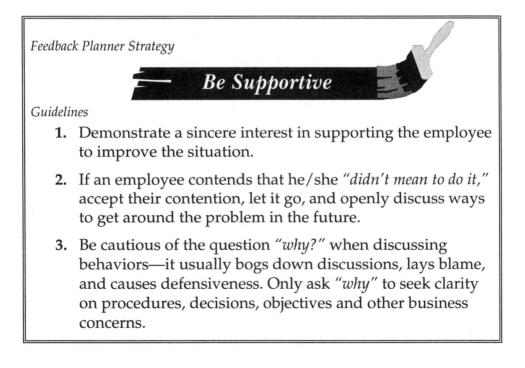

Feedback Planner Strategy

Be Supportive

Guidelines

1. Demonstrate a sincere interest in supporting the employee to improve the situation.

2. If an employee contends that he/she *"didn't mean to do it,"* accept their contention, let it go, and openly discuss ways to get around the problem in the future.

3. Be cautious of the question *"why?"* when discussing behaviors—it usually bogs down discussions, lays blame, and causes defensiveness. Only ask *"why"* to seek clarity on procedures, decisions, objectives and other business concerns.

CHAPTER FIVE WORKSHEET:
OVERCOMING COMMON OBSTACLES

Answer the following questions and apply the key learning points from Chapters Four and Five.

1. Identify an employee who primarily works in the field, on the road, at another site, or is otherwise not directly observable by you. How can you *"be factual with examples"* if you can't support your descriptions of their behaviors with direct observations?

_____

_____

_____

_____

_____

_____

_____

_____

_____

_____

2. You're the boss. Why isn't that a good enough reason by itself to impose your will on others and make them behave the way you want? Why shouldn't you impose your personal preferences for how you want your ship to be run?

_____

_____

_____

_____

_____

_____

3. Why is it a good idea to be cautious of the question _"why?"_ when discussing behaviors?

_____

_____

_____

_____

_____

_____

_____

_____

STAGE 4: IDENTIFY ALTERNATIVE BEHAVIORS

The Imposer

The Imposer mandates her opinions as if they were law—offers that can't be refused. Much like the Parent, she uses position power if she can to get her way. She tries to change behavior by jamming a solution down a person's throat to kill a discussion:

> *"You're not the most organized person I've worked with. Here. Use this system."*
>
> *"If you'd set your alarm to go off ten minutes earlier, you wouldn't be ten minutes late!"*
>
> *"You need to be a little more polished. I've signed you up for this class."*

As you probably noted, the Imposer's mandated solutions often follow a personal attack *(see the Attacker)* or a judgment *(see the Judge)*—the Imposer causes more problems than she solves!

If the imposed idea fails, the Imposer is usually blamed and a learning opportunity for both parties is lost. A failure doesn't inspire everyone to want to try again with an alternative plan. Imposed ideas are often sabotaged to fail to spite the Imposer.

If the imposed idea works, overdependency may result—the receiver loses an opportunity to think for himself. Or, there may be little to no understanding or commitment to the solution. The situation may improve temporarily, but a resentful receiver who didn't have a choice regarding the idea may not choose to change his behavior in the long run.

The Imposer catches . . .

Nick at his regional office: *"Nick, I want you to fly out to this upcoming management training program. I think it'll round out your skills a bit."*

Nick is confused, *"What program? And which skills need 'rounding'?"*

The Imposer beats around the bush for a while, then says, *"Look, Nick. It's not like you're a bad supervisor or anything. I just think you could learn to delegate a little more responsibility to your team. Stop hand-holding. You know."*

Nick was quick, *"No, I don't. Listen. I'm not saying I'm perfect or anything, but I've been to a lot of training programs. I've got four shelves of dusty binders to prove it! Tell me what you think I'm doing wrong and maybe we can work this out another way."*

The Imposer gets to the point: *"Nick, go to this program. Pick up what you can pick up, and we'll talk about it later, OK?"*

The Imposer should reel in her line and:

Feedback Planner Strategy

Be Encouraging And Offer Ideas

Guidelines

1. Encourage the employee to come up with alternative behaviors and action plans on his own. Let the employee retain responsibility for his current performance and be more committed to a plan he helped create.

2. Prepare to offer a few ideas of your own (*if you can't, how will the employee?*), in case he asks for help, *"tests you,"* or needs prodding.

The Quick Fixer

The Quick Fixer doesn't take much time to devise creative options for solving problems. He relies on old solutions—tried and simple remedies—to new and complex problems. If necessary, the Quick Fixer will even fit the situation to his solution! Whatever works *fast*:

> "Oh, yeah. I've seen this before. Here. Try this."
>
> "This is the way we've always done it. It should work for you."
>
> "All you have to do is this. What's the problem?!"

Sometimes the Quick Fixer may have a valid point. But if it's heard as the *only* or *final* point, it may not be heard at all.

The Quick Fixer listens anxiously . . .

to Barbara. *"The climate control system in our office is freezing me and Bev out of our minds. The vent blows directly on our desks all day. My fingers are numb. Is there anything we can do?"*

The Quick Fixer replies immediately, *"That's surprising. The system has always worked fine. My office is comfortable. Since we all have different needs and preferences, why don't you just wear sweaters?"*

Barbara is left in the cold, and walks off burning mad: *"Couldn't he contact his friend in the maintenance department to look at the system, adjust the vents, or have our desks moved to another location? Forget it. I'll do it myself. Knuckle head."*

The Quick Fixer should worry less about saving time and:

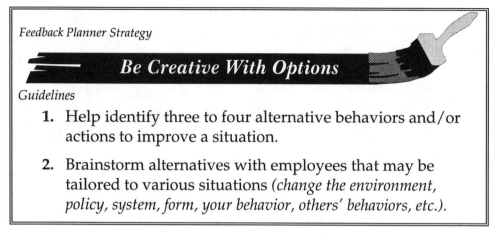

Feedback Planner Strategy

Be Creative With Options

Guidelines

1. Help identify three to four alternative behaviors and/or actions to improve a situation.

2. Brainstorm alternatives with employees that may be tailored to various situations (*change the environment, policy, system, form, your behavior, others' behaviors, etc.*).

The Abandoner

The Abandoner takes the responsibility of giving praise or criticism, and then runs from an obligation where her help may be most needed—suggesting ways to improve a situation:

"I know it's hard to accept what I just said. You'll get over it. You know what to do."

"You were dynamite! That project will open a lot of doors for you! Good luck!"

"You need to work on this skill. I know I'll see changes soon. I'm glad we had this talk."

Often, it takes a lot of time and effort to appropriately prepare and share criticism. Why, then, would the Abandoner leave others stranded without a plan? These receivers could go back to old behaviors, the situation may not change, they may need help and find none, etc.

Also, is our only reason to praise behavior to make others *"feel good"*? That's commendable, but certainly others *(and you)* would appreciate gaining *much more* by offering ways to capitalize on their strengths and the situation!

The Abandoner leaves . . .

Gary wondering how to get up to speed on the computer quickly. *"We'll have budgets coming out of our ears soon, and the Big Boss wants the whole process automated this year. I don't care what software you choose, as long as it's used. I trust you know what to do."*

Gary slowly responds, *"Uh, well, no. I mean, yes. Yes. Sure. Uh, thanks!"*

Gary runs back to his cubicle and grabs for his only hope—the training schedule from Computers-Are-Us. *"I'm dead. There's nothing scheduled that I need until next year."*

The Abandoner should stop walking away from opportunities for improvement and:

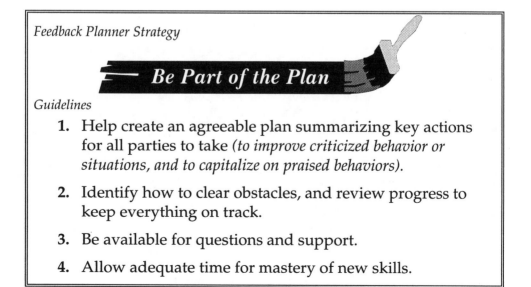

Feedback Planner Strategy

Be Part of the Plan

Guidelines

1. Help create an agreeable plan summarizing key actions for all parties to take *(to improve criticized behavior or situations, and to capitalize on praised behaviors)*.

2. Identify how to clear obstacles, and review progress to keep everything on track.

3. Be available for questions and support.

4. Allow adequate time for mastery of new skills.

The Pessimist

The Pessimist implies that something is inherently wrong with the employee or situation. New ideas won't work. She knows *(in her mind)* that the employee or situation cannot be changed:

> *"I've tried that before. It failed."*
>
> *"There's nothing you or I can do, except live with it."*
>
> *"Let's face it. That will never work. You can't teach an old dog new tricks."*

Nothing kills morale faster than a defeatist attitude.

The Pessimist finds fault . . .

with Joe's initial proposal to remodel the warehouse: *"It will cost too much money and take too much time."* Then the Pessimist serves up another 102 reasons why the idea will never fly. *"We recommended a similar plan two years ago, and it got eaten alive, along with the message carrier—me!"*

Joe reacts with his own volley: *"We lost our secondary storage space, so our raw materials are cluttering the aisles—not a safe situation. Also, since we've hired a new clerk, we're knocking into one another trying to access the computer jammed into the corner of the room. How much could it cost to get a few more shelves and cabinets, and reroute the computer terminal? We can do most of it ourselves. It's really no problem."*

The Pessimist returns with a backhanded smash: *"That's your opinion."*

The Pessimist should look for the light at the end of the tunnel and:

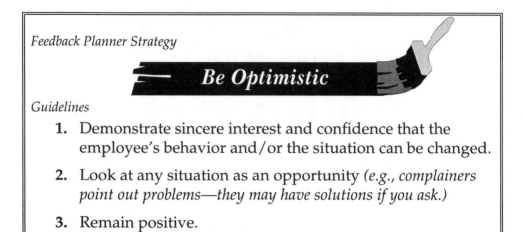

Feedback Planner Strategy

Be Optimistic

Guidelines

1. Demonstrate sincere interest and confidence that the employee's behavior and/or the situation can be changed.

2. Look at any situation as an opportunity (*e.g., complainers point out problems—they may have solutions if you ask.*)

3. Remain positive.

CHAPTER SIX WORKSHEET:
REMAINING OBJECTIVE
TO REDUCE OBJECTIONS

Answer the following questions and apply the key learning points from Chapter Six.

1. What are the pros and cons of imposing ideas on others?

PROS	CONS

2. Analyze a *"quick fix"* idea that you've had imposed on you to resolve an issue. What other creative options could have been discussed to improve your behavior and/or the situation?

_____

_____

_____

_____

_____

_____

_____

_____

3. Describe an example of feedback you've shared where your *"optimism"* helped to spur a change in the right direction.

_____

_____

_____

_____

_____

_____

_____

_____

CHAPTER SEVEN

UNDERSTANDING THE FEEDBACK PLANNER

Successful people don't let problems fester. They solve them before the trouble takes on a force of its own. These people also don't let a good thing go unnoticed. They look for more doors to open to get the most out of a situation. The Feedback Planner can be a key to your success.

Effective coaches develop the ability to objectively observe, analyze, and discuss a situation to gain involvement and commitment to improving it.

None of these skills is innate. The Feedback Planner will help build these skills—but not overnight. Using the Feedback Planner is like playing the piano. You not only need the tool—you need the practice!

The Goal

The Feedback Planner is an effective way to provide immediate feedback to reinforce *(through praise)* or redirect *(through criticism)* behavior to improve a situation.

The Purpose

The Feedback Planner is a note-taking worksheet that helps you collect and analyze your thoughts about a situation prior to discussing it with another person.

Its model below is simple, yet powerful.

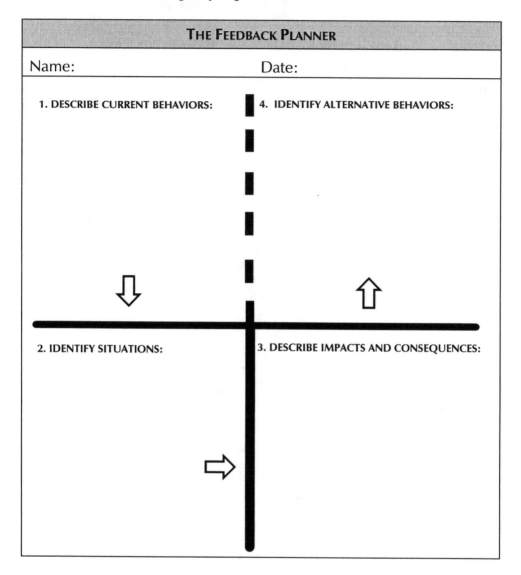

As you can see, the Feedback Planner is composed of four boxes. Each is available for you to take notes on what you may say during the four stages of the feedback process.

Here are the Feedback Planner's basic form and guidelines:

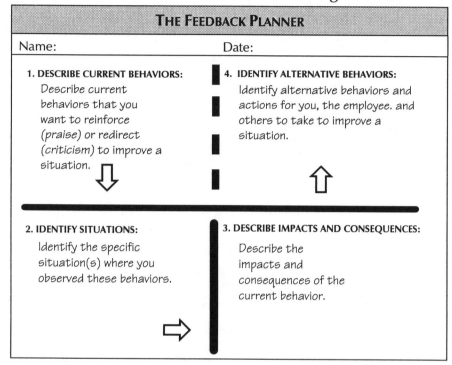

How To Use The Feedback Planner

The best way to learn how to play piano is to touch the keys. The best way to learn how to use the Feedback Planner is to fill it out.

Step 1—Collect your thoughts

Take a blank Feedback Planner and collect all of your initial thoughts about a person's behavior and a situation by noting them in the appropriate boxes of the Planner. You don't have to fill in the boxes in any particular order. Jot down ideas as they randomly occur. You can complete and revise your notes later.

Step 2—Complete your thoughts

Look for *"holes"* in your Feedback Planner. Have you described the specific behavior in Box 1? Have you identified two to three examples of situations in Box 2? Have you described six to ten impacts/consequences in Box 3? Have you identified three to four alternative behaviors and/or actions in Box 4? At this step, you are going for *quantity* of information.

Step 3—Revise your thoughts

Use the Feedback Planner strategies discussed in Chapters Three through Six to analyze and revise your notes. These strategies are listed below in the appropriate feedback stages *(and boxes)*. At this step, you are going for *quality* of information.

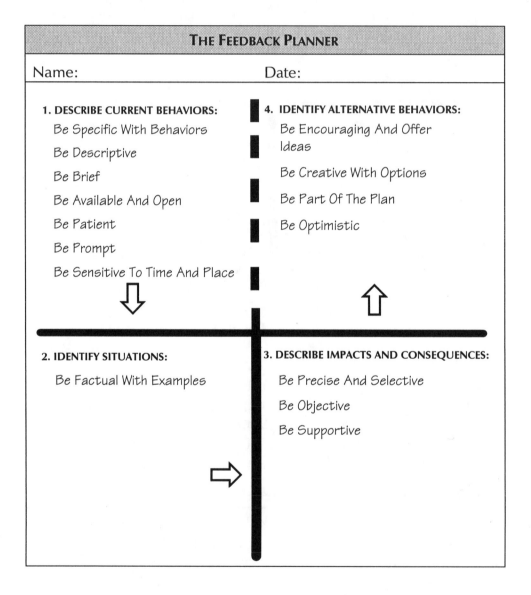

THE FEEDBACK PLANNER	
Name:	Date:

1. DESCRIBE CURRENT BEHAVIORS:
- Be Specific With Behaviors
- Be Descriptive
- Be Brief
- Be Available And Open
- Be Patient
- Be Prompt
- Be Sensitive To Time And Place

4. IDENTIFY ALTERNATIVE BEHAVIORS:
- Be Encouraging And Offer Ideas
- Be Creative With Options
- Be Part Of The Plan
- Be Optimistic

2. IDENTIFY SITUATIONS:
- Be Factual With Examples

3. DESCRIBE IMPACTS AND CONSEQUENCES:
- Be Precise And Selective
- Be Objective
- Be Supportive

Step 4—Discuss your thoughts

Your notes can act as a helpful script to keep you on track during the face-to-face session. You can also keep these notes as a documentation of your discussion.

Giving a copy of your notes to the receiver can be very beneficial. It shows that you care about the person and the situation by taking the time to collect and analyze your thoughts. It shows that you don't have any hidden agendas. It shows that you are open to others' views. And, it helps to focus the discussion on an objective analysis of the situation—in a sense, it depersonalizes it.

Revising your notes with the receiver's input demonstrates that you are not set in your views. An open and frank discussion equalizes your relationship—you are working together on equal ground trying to understand and improve a situation.

Understanding The "Boxes"

 Describe current behaviors

It's important here to build agreement and understanding. People filter behaviors through their own points-of-view, which is natural, but often subjective and incomplete. Box 1 of the Feedback Planner provides the foundation for a mutually agreed upon and understood perspective of the current behavior. *(See how "perceptions" may fit Box 3.)*

Be Descriptive; **NOT JUDGMENTAL**

Words can build up or destroy. The ones you choose will determine the outcome of your encounter. Loaded and inflammatory language *(which tends to arouse feelings of anger or other strong emotions)*—"poor attitude," "foolish mistake," "sweet disposition"—will undermine your objective: To positively influence behavior and situations.

If you judge someone as having a *"bad attitude,"* the person will likely defend himself to the exclusion of all else. This leads to a verbal tennis match—*"Yes, you do." "No, I don't." "Yes, you do." "No, I don't."*—which as everyone knows, leads nowhere.

The following conversations show how judgmental words can hurt a discussion or relationship, and descriptive words can improve a situation.

Conversation A
JUDGMENTAL

Boss: *"You are a poor team player." (Box 1 Attacker)*

Employee: *"No I'm not."*

Boss: *"Yes, you are. You never volunteer for special assignments in our staff meetings." (Box 2 Fabricator)*

Employee: *"I've been swamped with work. I don't want to say 'yes' to additional work and then let the team down. And now you're telling me I'm a poor team player? That's not what I meant when I said 'no'."*

Boss: *"You must have. Otherwise you wouldn't have said it." (Box 3 Psychologist)*

Analysis:

The boss starts with an unsubstantiated attack. He does not accept the employee's explanation as true. Then he causes the employee to be defensive by implying that the employee is a liar. So much for objectivity. So much for Psychology 101.

Conversation B

Descriptive

(Using the Feedback Planner strategies)

Boss: *"In our last three meetings (Box 2 Situations), you didn't volunteer for any of the special assignments our team had to accept one way or another (Box 1 Current Behavior). Some members, including myself, believe we have shouldered more than our fair share." (Box 3 Impacts)*

Employee: *"I can't believe it. That's not what I meant when I said 'no.'"*

Boss: *"I didn't think so. I'm glad I came to you. What's going on?"*

Employee: *"I've been swamped with work. I didn't want to say I'll take on an additional assignment, and then let you and the team down."*

Boss: *"That makes sense. And, yet, we still need to respond to these drop-in's as a team."*

Employee: *"Yes I know."*

Boss: *"Let's talk about what you and I can do differently in the future."* *(Box 4 Alternative Behaviors)*

Analysis:

The boss focused on the employee's behavior, using specific situations and impacts to support the boss' concern. The boss diminished defensiveness by sticking to the facts and not veering into a personal attack. The boss equalized the playing field by acknowledging the employee's position and inviting the employee to explain further. By asking, *"What's going on?"* the boss opened channels of communication. After listening to the employee's explanation, the boss joined the employee in devising options to improve the situation.

Box 2 — Identify situations

Don't wait three weeks or three months to deal with a situation. Step away from it just long enough to use the Feedback Planner. Box 2 confines the current behavior to a time and place.

Sure, you can't always be there to observe each and every behavior. You'd be accused of being a *"backseat driver"!* But you can collect and share facts, figures, and other important information from written sources. . . .

WRITTEN SOURCES	
• activity reports	• performance plans
• business plans	• performance standards
• calendars	• personnel records
• charts and graphics	• policies and procedures
• *"critical incident"* files	• project charts and schedules
• customer complaint letters	• project status reports
• customer letters of commendation	• proposals and contracts
• employee self evaluations	• strategic goals, objectives, and tactics
• feedback forms	• surveys
• job descriptions	• time sheets
• operating manuals and references	• your personal notes
• past performance appraisals	

. . . and you can collect and share observations and perceptions from others with interviews:

INTERVIEWS	
• clients	• internal suppliers *(e.g., other employees)*
• consultants	
• contractors	• managers
• coworkers	• past supervisors
• external customers	• supervisors
• external suppliers	• the employee
• internal customers *(e.g., department users)*	• witnesses to *"critical incidents"*

Chapter Eight will demonstrate how the Feedback Planner can be used as an interview tool to collect facts, figures, observations, and perceptions.

Box 3   **Describe impacts and consequences**

This box is the crux of the Feedback Planner. Box 3 spurs behavior change—it justifies and *sells* the need for change.

Consequences are among the most powerful of motivators. Most people don't quit smoking because they want to. They quit smoking because they will likely get lung cancer and die.

Every behavior, action, or situation has impacts and consequences that affect more than a single entity. The more specific you can be in describing impacts, the more likely you will spur change. Brainstorm six to ten impacts and consequences at first, and then select three or four of the most critical, attention-grabbing and convincing ones through the eyes and ears of the receiver. *"Sell"* the need for change.

Use perceptions cautiously

How other people perceive an employee's behavior is fair game in discussing impacts of this behavior as long as perceptions are appropriately described in Box 3 *and not judged in Box 1.* This will also help you to avoid the *"Yes, you are. No, I'm not."* trap.

Notice the differences:

Box 1 CURRENT BEHAVIORS JUDGMENTAL	Box 3 IMPACTS AND CONSEQUENCES Descriptive
"You are offensive."	*"Your comments were offensive to me and the staff."*
"You are disorganized."	*"Our customers can view your office as disorganized."*
"You have a bad attitude."	*"You seem angry to me."*
"You are a poor team player."	*"I'm not comfortable asking you for help."*

Note: A natural defense to *"You are offensive"* is *"No, I'm not."* Yet, the employee *can't* respond to *"Your comments were offensive to me and the staff"* with *"No, they weren't."* A likely defense may be *"I didn't mean to be offensive,"* and a recommended response would be *"Fine. I'm glad we're talking about this to clear the air."*

Perceptions equal reality to the person who has them. A strong word of caution, however. You may find perceptions easy and plentiful to list at first in Box 3, but you will see that perceptions often do not have the same weight as other impacts and consequences. See Chapter Five for more guidelines.

Equalize The Relationship

When you begin to describe impacts and consequences, employees may attempt to clarify their position—*"I didn't mean that."* Don't delve into the reasons why an employee did this or that, unless you *really are* a paid psychologist. It hardens defenses and bogs down the feedback process.

If the employee says he didn't mean to do it or was misunderstood, whether you believe it or not, accept the explanation and move on to your objective: ways to improve the behavior or situation.

Turn the defense to both of your advantages. Allow the employee to save face—*"Well, then, I'm glad we're talking about this"* or, *"I didn't think so. That's why I came to you to discuss it."* This lays the groundwork for two-way communication and teamwork, which you'll need for Box 4.

JUSTIFY YOUR FEEDBACK

Another important feature of Box 3 is that it forces you to gauge the seriousness of the impacts and consequences of the current behavior *(in essence, justify your feedback).*

If you get to Box 3 and the only impact you can think of is *"I don't like it,"* then the problem may lie with you, not the employee. Review your analysis and make sure it's not your own intolerance that is at the root of the problem. You may not be *justified* in giving this feedback.

Box 4

Identify alternative behaviors

This is your chance to mutually generate creative options.
Box 4 is where problems with undesirable behavior *(being criticized)* are creatively solved, and benefits with desirable behavior *(being praised)* are reinforced and capitalized on. Don't blow it here by imposing solutions!

Imposed solutions are often ineffective because they are one-sided, and they usually lay blame squarely at the feet of the employee. They imply that the employee is the only part of the situation that needs to be changed. It's better to address the issue—whether it is a behavior or situation—in all its facets. Almost always, there is more than one way to improve a situation.

Be creative as you generate alternative behaviors together. Following is a selected list of options that may help you finalize a plan for Box 4 Alternative Behaviors.

Box 4 DEVELOPMENT OPTIONS	EXPLANATION
1. Job enrichment	Delegate more authority, autonomy, etc., in the employee's current role.
2. Job enlargement	Assign additional responsibilities to the current role.
3. On-the-job coaching	Impart skills, knowledge, and direction to develop the employee.
4. Special assignment	Provide for comprehensive research of a problem to enhance technical skills.
5. Job rotation or transfer	Move the employee to another job to broaden experience and perspective.
6. Substitute assignment	Let the employee temporarily assume responsibilities for others who are on vacation, traveling, on a leave of absence, etc.
7. Understudy	Have the employee work directly with another to eventually be a replacement.
8. Mentorship	Allow the employee to periodically *"interview"* specialists to enhance aptitude.
9. Leadership opportunity	Let the employee lead meetings, presentations, task forces, etc.
10. Training assignment	Arrange for cross-training to build credibility and confidence.
11. Study materials	Provide manuals, videos, cassettes, and other self-study reference materials, and follow-up to reinforce learning.
12. Professional development programs	Let the employee attend conferences and workshops to develop specific skills and networks.

CHAPTER SEVEN WORKSHEET: PLANNING FOR FEEDBACK

Answer the following questions and apply the key learning points from Chapter Seven.

1. What are the benefits to eventually *giving a copy* of your Feedback Planner notes to the receiver, and *revising* your notes with the receiver's input?

_____

_____

_____

_____

2. Identify one praise and one criticism you want to share with another person. Write each twice—be *Judgmental* and be *Descriptive*. This practice will help you recognize and choose to stay on the right track.

FEEDBACK	JUDGMENTAL	DESCRIPTIVE
Praise		
Criticism		

3. In your own words, what is the main purpose of Box 3? How can you capitalize on its use?

_____

_____

_____

4. Describe how a person's *perceptions* were inappropriately shared with you. Why should you be cautious of your use of perceptions in Box 3?

_____

_____

5. Identify a solution that has been imposed on you, and your reaction. Was the *imposed solution* effective or ineffective? Why? How should this solution have been brought to your attention? Why?

_____

_____

_____

6. Which *"development options"* in Box 4 do you and your team use most to improve performance on the job? Least? Which are most and least effective? Why?

_____

_____

_____

USING THE FEEDBACK PLANNER

The Feedback Planner is versatile. Read through the following seven scenarios to see the Feedback Planner in use. Then try a few of your own. Adapt the model to meet your needs.

1. Boss Praises Employee

Note: The Feedback Planner can help Mike capitalize on Jennifer's positive behavior and bring his praise of her to life.

Jennifer was working late ...

when she received an urgent call from the printer. The front section of the client publication was missing. Was it not sent? Did the printer misplace it? There was no time or need for blame—just barely enough time to fix the problem. This wasn't Jennifer's project and there was no one to ask at that time of night.

Jennifer unsuccessfully tried to call her boss, Mike, and her coworkers who were assigned to this client. She told the printer to hold on while she rebuilt the section based on some past drafts she found.

Jennifer spent the next two hours putting the publication back in shape. She delivered it to the printer 20 miles away and waited until the job was finished before heading home. The next morning, the project was delivered two hours early to the client.

Mike looked into the matter, found out about the details, and noted his discoveries on the Feedback Planner to praise Jennifer.

Mike's Feedback Planner:

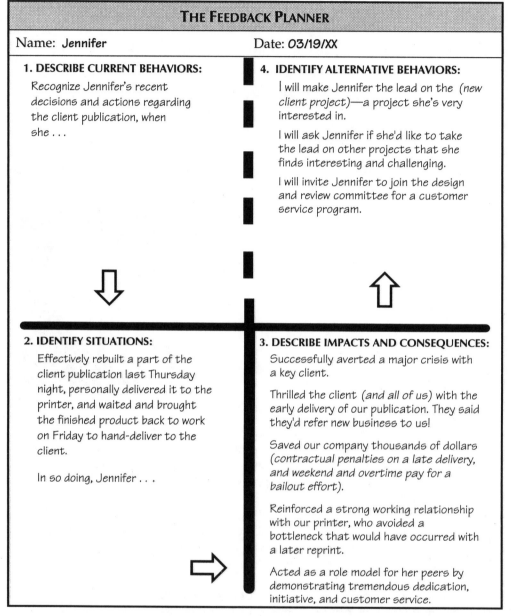

THE FEEDBACK PLANNER

Name: *Jennifer*   Date: *03/19/XX*

1. DESCRIBE CURRENT BEHAVIORS:

Recognize Jennifer's recent decisions and actions regarding the client publication, when she . . .

4. IDENTIFY ALTERNATIVE BEHAVIORS:

I will make Jennifer the lead on the *(new client project)*—a project she's very interested in.

I will ask Jennifer if she'd like to take the lead on other projects that she finds interesting and challenging.

I will invite Jennifer to join the design and review committee for a customer service program.

2. IDENTIFY SITUATIONS:

Effectively rebuilt a part of the client publication last Thursday night, personally delivered it to the printer, and waited and brought the finished product back to work on Friday to hand-deliver to the client.

In so doing, Jennifer . . .

3. DESCRIBE IMPACTS AND CONSEQUENCES:

Successfully averted a major crisis with a key client.

Thrilled the client *(and all of us)* with the early delivery of our publication. They said they'd refer new business to us!

Saved our company thousands of dollars *(contractual penalties on a late delivery, and weekend and overtime pay for a bailout effort)*.

Reinforced a strong working relationship with our printer, who avoided a bottleneck that would have occurred with a later reprint.

Acted as a role model for her peers by demonstrating tremendous dedication, initiative, and customer service.

Alternative to avoid:

Mike to Jennifer: *"I heard you worked all night on the client publication. Thanks! You really bailed us out. I'll be talking with Cindy and Liz tomorrow so you won't have to pick up their missing pieces again. Sorry for ruining your night."*

2. Employee Criticizes Boss

Note: The Feedback Planner can help equalize a situation between Sean and his boss, Joan. The Planner also can be used to *"script"* a conversation to help you practice what you actually want to say in critical and sensitive situations.

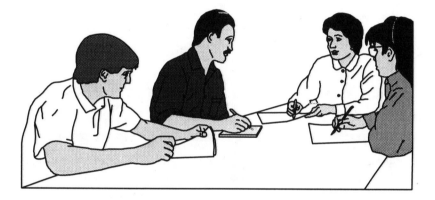

Sean collects his initial thoughts . . .

"Joan's meetings can be a rambling and unfocused waste of time. Finger pointers have turned the meetings into witch hunts and gripe sessions. Occasionally, a shouting match erupts. Last week, a staff meeting ran on for three hours. Three of us were late for other appointments."

He decided to use the Feedback Planner to script what he may actually say to Joan.

Sean's Feedback Planner:

THE FEEDBACK PLANNER	
Name: Joan	**Date: 11/04/XX**

1. DESCRIBE CURRENT BEHAVIORS:

Joan, I'd like to talk with you about our staff meetings.

Currently, you're juggling the load of meeting leader, facilitator, note taker, and participant.

As you told me yesterday, your workload doesn't allow you to do what you want to do—provide an agenda, keep our discussions focused, etc.

⇩

4. IDENTIFY ALTERNATIVE BEHAVIORS:

These meetings should not be cancelled—they are necessary. But, we need to take better advantage of the time together.

We could rotate the roles of meeting leader, facilitator, note taker, and/or participant.

A facilitator could set ground rules to manage our time, processes, and expected behaviors per the leader's agenda.

I can draft an agenda for your review before our next meeting.

What do you think? What else can I do to help? ⇧

2. IDENTIFY SITUATIONS:

In our last four meetings on (dates and times, as necessary), most of us were able to spend considerable time on our personal issues without time constraints or team buy-in. We went over our schedule (times).

Sometimes our emotions got to the best of us . . .(refers to the recent shouting match in the last meeting).

⇨

3. DESCRIBE IMPACTS AND CONSEQUENCES:

Without an agreed-upon purpose, others can perceive some discussions as unfocused or inappropriate.

Without the proper guidance and preparation, problem-solving efforts have covered old ground repeatedly. Some of us have missed critical information and opportunities.

Unmanaged arguments have caused some of us to feel a sense of failure.

Long meetings take us away from more pressing issues and appointments.

Alternative to avoid:

Do nothing. Complain to everyone but Joan. Sit back and let the meetings *(and your life)* expire. Skip the meeting. You should realize that all of these responses reinforce the status quo!

3. Employee Criticizes Coworker

Note: Suzanne's initial thoughts *(subjective and loaded)* can be *"filtered"* by the structure and strategies of the Feedback Planner. The Feedback Planner can be adapted to meet Suzanne's needs as she prepares to talk with a coworker, Peter. *(Often, Box 2 has only a few phrases. In the example below, Suzanne found it more effective to itemize and connect Box 2 Situations with Box 3 Impacts And Consequences.)*

Suzanne vents her initial thoughts
(with the author's analysis):

"Peter is disorganized."	Box 1 Attacker
"I've been wanting to tell him this for months."	Box 1 Laggard
"His desk is always an embarrassing mess and a headache for all of us."	Box 2 Fabricator
"I can only imagine what his room looked like as a kid . . . "	Box 3 Psychologist
"If I could just get him to use Shelly's filing system . . . "	Box 4 Quick Fixer
"Or, we can just accept him as he is, and surround this eyesore with large office plants . . . "	Box 4 Pessimist

Suzanne knows she's a bit heated and has some work to do. She gets out a Feedback Planner. . . .

Suzanne's Feedback Planner:

THE FEEDBACK PLANNER	
Name: **Peter**	Date: **05/22/XX**

1. DESCRIBE CURRENT BEHAVIORS:

Peter, I'd like to talk with you about the way you currently manage the paperwork in your cubicle, on your desk, and in your file drawers . . .

⬇

4. IDENTIFY ALTERNATIVE BEHAVIORS:

Since we are all not always at our desks and need access to each other's files, we need to be able to secure and quickly locate necessary documents to meet our deadlines.

Our open cubicles must give a favorable impression to our visitors.

Have you had similar issues or concerns?

Do you have any suggestions?

Shelly suggested this system . . . (share in detail). Could you label your stacks with post-it notes?

Do you need more filing cabinets? Could you rearrange your office?

⬆

2. IDENTIFY SITUATIONS:

A. When you were out on vacation, neither John nor I could quickly find several client files and reports—specifically the (files/reports).

B. On (dates and times), you were four and six dates late submitting your (reports) because you told us you couldn't locate some pertinent records I left with you.

C. Since your desk is in an open cubicle in a high traffic area, customers can see it easily as they walk by.

➡

3. DESCRIBE IMPACTS AND CONSEQUENCES:

A. John had to recreate one of the reports, causing rework. I found the other after several hours of searching, causing downtime.

B. Some of these misplaced documents cannot be replaced, and our monthly deadlines cannot continue to be missed. Other departments count on these timely reports.

C. A desk and open file drawers with scattered papers may give our customers the impression that we're disorganized.

Alternative to avoid:

Suzanne *(Box 1 Hit-And-Run)*: *"Please clean up your act, will ya, Peter?"*
Peter answers, *"Say what?!"*

4. Employee Praises Coworker

Here's a second quick example of adapting the Feedback Planner to meet your needs. This time, Debbie is giving praise to Wendy. We've divided the conversation into the Planner's Boxes.

THE FEEDBACK PLANNER	
Name: **Wendy**	Date: **02/13/XX**

1. DESCRIBE CURRENT BEHAVIORS:

Wendy, I'd like to compliment your work on our team "Project ABC" *(followed with specific behaviors).*

4. IDENTIFY ALTERNATIVE BEHAVIORS:

Leading *(a new project team)* could be a great opportunity for you to show others your talents. Senior management is pushing for this *(new project).* Are you interested? Just talk to our supervisor. I'll support you!

Do you have other projects you're interested in? Maybe I can help open some doors by putting in a good word for you!

⇩   ⇧

2. IDENTIFY SITUATIONS:

A. I know you have put a lot of your own time and effort in completing the project.

B. Sue *(the project leader)* tells me you really add value to her meetings by participating actively and by encouraging others to participate. We all feel the same!

C. You haven't missed a beat completing your other work and lending a hand *(e.g., you helped me redesign the project budget).*

⇨

3. DESCRIBE IMPACTS AND CONSEQUENCES:

A. I have heard several comments from senior management about how much better the process works since you've taken over!

B. You're really becoming a leader. You are gaining respect from others around the company. You certainly have my vote!

C. Because of the successful implementations of the improvements you suggested, the Finance Department is changing the budget format company-wide. Thanks!

5. Boss Criticizes Employee And Situation

Note: The Feedback Planner can be used to collect and discuss a situation *"live."* The Planner can also keep a relationship between Greg and Jeff intact even when Greg, the provider of the feedback, has an incomplete or inaccurate picture.

Greg's initial thoughts:

Greg has scheduled a meeting to talk with Jeff about a recent incident with a customer that he heard about *(but did not observe)*. Greg picked up this much so far from Jeff's coworkers who approached Greg with the unsolicited *"inside scoop"*:

Jeff was handling the counter at the office products store. He was processing a return item from a lady when she blew up. As one of Jeff's coworkers put it: *"She apparently wanted her money back on a purchase. I don't know what Jeff said, but she yelled at everyone and stormed out of the store with her merchandise. He must have pressed the wrong buttons and really got on her nerves!"*

Greg had little else to work with, so he collected his sketchy picture on the Feedback Planner and approached Jeff. . . .

Greg's Feedback Planner:

Note: See the question marks and *"unknowns"* in parentheses. When in doubt about a situation, use the Planner to collect more information.

THE FEEDBACK PLANNER

Name: **Jeff**   Date: **08/17/XX**

1. DESCRIBE CURRENT BEHAVIORS:

Jeff, I'd like to talk with you about how you handled a particular situation with a customer yesterday. I don't have the whole picture on exactly what happened.

4. IDENTIFY ALTERNATIVE BEHAVIORS:

(Since I don't have enough information, I don't know whether Jeff can do something differently in the future. Maybe it's a problem with our policy? Could I do something to help?)

2. IDENTIFY SITUATIONS:

I'm referring to a lady you helped while handling the counter about 3:00 P.M. yesterday afternoon? Do you know who I'm referring to?

(Jeff says: "Yes").

Apparently, this customer approached you about wanting her money back on some merchandise, and then left with her merchandise? She may have been upset?

Is this true? What happened?

3. DESCRIBE IMPACTS AND CONSEQUENCES:

(Something caused a customer to leave with merchandise she apparently wanted to return?)

(The customer was upset?)

(Other employees and customers were affected?)

Jeff's response helped Greg add to his Feedback Planner:

THE FEEDBACK PLANNER

Name: Jeff   **Date:** 08/17/XX

1. DESCRIBE CURRENT BEHAVIORS:

Jeff: "I asked the customer to take a brief moment to fill out the proper paperwork for returning merchandise, and said that I'd be happy to refund her money immediately."

Jeff's behavior was according to company policy.

4. IDENTIFY ALTERNATIVE BEHAVIORS:

Simplify the paperwork, fill it out for the customer, or eliminate the need for it by changing the policy to better accommodate customer needs.

Establish a special and separate location for returns, exchanges or refunds. Designate an employee to handle this responsibility.

Jeff could ask the customer for permission to help someone else while the paperwork is being filled out (as a sign of courtesy).

Staff extra help during busy periods. Jeff should use the intercom to call for help immediately as often as necessary.

The entire team could revisit the guidelines for when to call for help, and how quickly the help should respond.

2. IDENTIFY SITUATIONS:

Jeff: "As she began, I started to help the next customer in line. There was a line of five customers and no help in sight. I didn't call for help. It usually takes too long for someone to arrive."

"The lady became frustrated and yelled at this customer behind her for 'cutting in'. When a scene began between the two of them, this lady just ran out."

"I think she was frustrated or embarrassed, or something. Maybe she didn't want to hold everyone up any more than I did."

3. DESCRIBE IMPACTS AND CONSEQUENCES:

Jeff: "I felt bad about the whole thing. So did Mrs. Johnson, the customer behind her. She said she'd be available to help explain what happened."

The customer left unsatisfied with her unwanted merchandise and no refund. She will likely never return and will tell all her friends.

Other customers witnessed an unhappy customer. They could misinterpret what happened and form a negative impression on Jeff and the store.

Our return and refund/exchange policies may be seen by our customers as needlessly complex, inflexible, or "non-value-added."

Alternative to avoid:

Imagine if Greg had jumped to a conclusion and said, *"Jeff, I don't care what your side of the story is—the customer is always right. You said something to get this lady to blow up and storm out. I have witnesses. Customers don't just do that unless they're provoked. Do you realize just how devastating this can be to our business?! And your job? What's gotten into you lately?"*

"A knife in my back," thinks Greg.

6. Boss (Almost) Criticizes Employee (By Mistake)

Note: The Feedback Planner can help point out that some feedback you may feel a need to give may not be justified, regardless of your position, authority, etc.

Bruce prepares to criticize . . .

He is disappointed with the way Linda is handling customer calls. Linda has been on Bruce's sales staff for six months now. Linda had two years of successful experience in a similar sales function prior to joining Bruce's team. . . .

Bruce's Feedback Planner:

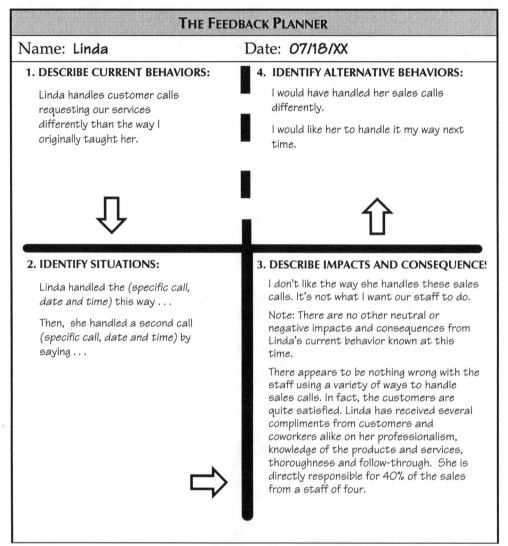

THE FEEDBACK PLANNER

Name: **Linda**   Date: **07/18/XX**

1. DESCRIBE CURRENT BEHAVIORS:

Linda handles customer calls requesting our services differently than the way I originally taught her.

4. IDENTIFY ALTERNATIVE BEHAVIORS:

I would have handled her sales calls differently.

I would like her to handle it my way next time.

2. IDENTIFY SITUATIONS:

Linda handled the (specific call, date and time) this way . . .

Then, she handled a second call (specific call, date and time) by saying . . .

3. DESCRIBE IMPACTS AND CONSEQUENCES

I don't like the way she handles these sales calls. It's not what I want our staff to do.

Note: There are no other neutral or negative impacts and consequences from Linda's current behavior known at this time.

There appears to be nothing wrong with the staff using a variety of ways to handle sales calls. In fact, the customers are quite satisfied. Linda has received several compliments from customers and coworkers alike on her professionalism, knowledge of the products and services, thoroughness and follow-through. She is directly responsible for 40% of the sales from a staff of four.

Alternative to avoid:

Bruce to Linda: *"This is my ship and I'll choose to run it the way I want. From now on, I want you to . . . "*

Linda is looking for a life preserver as she walks down the gangplank. . . .

Note: If the impacts and consequences had been different, Bruce may have been justified to discuss and require alternative behaviors from Linda (*e.g., details have slipped through the cracks; coworkers have not followed through on others' commitments due to poor pass-offs; etc.*). But this isn't the case here.

CHAPTER EIGHT WORKSHEET:
APPLYING THE FEEDBACK PLANNER
ON THE JOB

Apply the key learning points from Chapter Eight. Identify an employee with whom you would like to share feedback *(criticism or praise)*. Follow the first three steps below to demonstrate your use of the Feedback Planner.

Step 1—Collect Your Thoughts

Use the blank Feedback Planner on the next page to collect and note all of your initial thoughts *(about this person's behavior and the situation)*.

Step 2—Complete Your Thoughts

Have you described the specific behavior in Box 1? Have you identified two to three examples of situations in Box 2? Have you described six to ten impacts/consequences in Box 3? Have you identified three to four alternative behaviors and/or actions in Box 4?

Step 3—Revise Your Thoughts

Use the Feedback Planner strategies discussed in Chapters Three through Six to analyze and revise your notes.

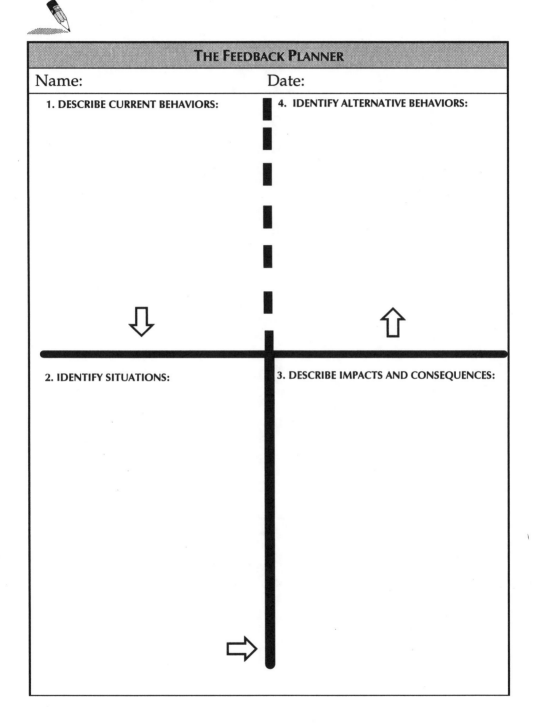

THE FEEDBACK PLANNER

Name: Date:

1. DESCRIBE CURRENT BEHAVIORS:

4. IDENTIFY ALTERNATIVE BEHAVIORS:

2. IDENTIFY SITUATIONS:

3. DESCRIBE IMPACTS AND CONSEQUENCES:

REFINING THE FEEDBACK PLANNER WITH STYLE

Assessing Your Communication Style

Communication style should play an important role when you revise and share your thoughts using the Feedback Planner. Your efforts will be more effective if you are aware of your own and the receiver's preferred communication style, including strengths, weaknesses, and preferences.

There are four major communication styles. The styles are:

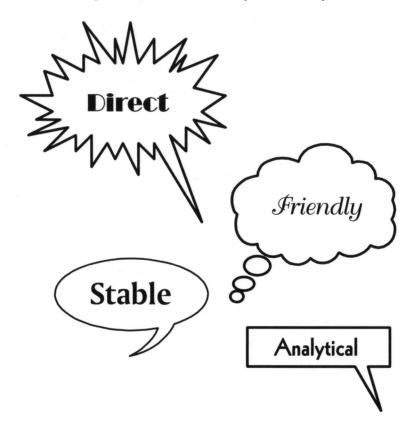

Most people's communication styles are a composite of all four styles, but everyone has a preferred style.

Direct

STRENGTHS SHARING FEEDBACK	WEAKNESSES SHARING FEEDBACK	PREFERENCES RECEIVING FEEDBACK
• Confident • Takes charge • Clear, to the point, direct • Decisive • Pragmatic • Results-oriented • Determined • Outspoken • Risk taker • Challenging	• Too brief, blunt • Dominates • Listens poorly • Inspires fear, burnout • Impatient, insensitive • Too quick • Intimidating	• Be prepared, brief, direct • Present facts logically, efficiently *(in "bullets")* • Focus on objectives, results, probability of success • Focus on what *(not how)* • Ask *"what"* questions to get their input quickly • Provide options for them to choose, be in charge • Recognize their accomplishments • Stick to business, depart graciously

Friendly

STRENGTHS SHARING FEEDBACK	WEAKNESSES SHARING FEEDBACK	PREFERENCES RECEIVING FEEDBACK
• Talkative • Approachable • Motivational • Enthusiastic • Persuasive • Successful with and through others • Optimistic • Generous • Friendly, sociable, trusting, popular • Poised, confident	• Oversells ideas • Unprepared, unclear • Misses details, follow-through • Too sensitive, trusting, emotional • Too agreeable, makes promises just to be liked • Impulsive • Self-promoting to a fault	• Be democratic, upbeat, stimulating, fast-moving, conversational • Share goals without details • Ask for their opinions and visions • Suggest implementation plans • Use *"credible"* testimonials to sell • Offer incentives for action • Provide public recognition • Leave time for socializing

Stable

STRENGTHS SHARING FEEDBACK	WEAKNESSES SHARING FEEDBACK	PREFERENCES RECEIVING FEEDBACK
• Sincere, trustworthy • Patient, persistent • Listens actively • Calm, easy-going, steady • Depends on proven processes • Deliberate • Loyal • Team player • Considerate, sympathetic • Procedure-oriented (asks "how?")	• Avoids confrontations • Too patient, yielding, giving of false hopes • Too quiet, restrained, passive, taken advantage of • Slow to change • Holds grudges • Possessive • Risk-aversive to a fault	• Be sincere, personable, agreeable, supportive • Provide plans and suggestions in advance • Present calmly, nonthreateningly • Focus on what and how • Clearly define roles, goals, expectations • Minimize risks, unknowns • Be patient, give time to think, respond, adjust • Follow-up for thoughts, questions, concerns

Analytical

STRENGTHS SHARING FEEDBACK	WEAKNESSES SHARING FEEDBACK	PREFERENCES RECEIVING FEEDBACK
• Thorough, well-prepared • Accurate • Objective, logical • Controlled, cautious • Systematic • Detail-oriented • Precise with expectations • Plans to reduce risks • Challenges "why?" • Organized, neat	• Insensitive, too critical • Inflexible, misses big picture • Withdrawn, nontrusting • Imposes high standards • Too cautious, worry-wart • Controlling • Perfectionist	• Be thoroughly logical, objective, patient, persistent • Present "big picture" and specifics • Focus on what and why • List pros/cons to options, and contingencies • Support everything with data • Solicit input, criticisms and changes • Develop detailed implementation plans together • Follow-up for verification, improvements

"Flexing" Your Style To Reach Others

There were several strategies outlined in Chapters Three through Six that provide an opportunity for you to apply this valuable information on communication styles. They will help you provide more effective feedback.

The following four Feedback Planner Box examples should give you a general idea of how to refine your Feedback Planner with style (*keep in mind that there are many more opportunities beyond those outlined below!*):

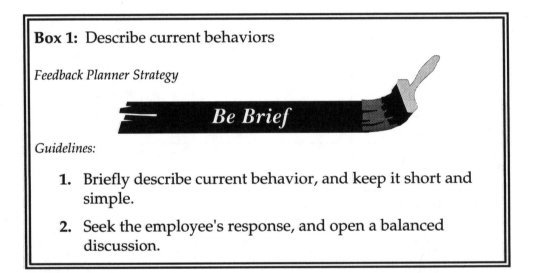

Box 1: Describe current behaviors

Feedback Planner Strategy

Be Brief

Guidelines:

1. Briefly describe current behavior, and keep it short and simple.

2. Seek the employee's response, and open a balanced discussion.

Here's how to *"flex"* your communication styles when giving feedback:

Direct and *Friendly:* These people won't give you much time—they'll interrupt if you're long-winded. Get right to the point, focus on the *"what's,"* not the *"how's,"* and get them talking! They won't be shy.

Stable and Analytical: Be patient and expect silence at first. They may be threatened by your criticism and weary of your praise. Prepare questions to get them involved. Focus on the *"how's"* and the *"why's."*

Analytical: Remain poised for countercriticisms and questions.

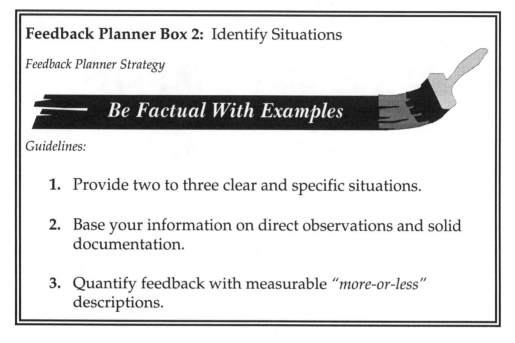

Feedback Planner Box 2: Identify Situations

Feedback Planner Strategy

Be Factual With Examples

Guidelines:

1. Provide two to three clear and specific situations.

2. Base your information on direct observations and solid documentation.

3. Quantify feedback with measurable *"more-or-less"* descriptions.

Here's how to *"flex"* your communication styles:

Direct: Be brief and expect them to do the same. If you've done your job, they'll have little to share except reasons. Quickly move to Boxes 3 and 4.

Friendly: Allow time to hear an earful. They want to make sure you still like them!

Stable: Expect to get some *"uh huh's"* or the *"Bambi-Stare"*—big eyes, head tilted, silence, tentative look, ready-to-dart posture. They're just collecting their thoughts and waiting for you to continue. Move on.

Analytical: Be prepared with lots of facts, and patient as they look for something you left out. They'll find it.

Feedback Planner Box 3: Describe impacts and consequences

Feedback Planner Strategy

Be Precise and Selective

Guidelines:

1. Identify six to ten precise impacts on business operations and consequences.

2. Select the three to four that will get the receiver's attention.

Brainstorming six to ten or more impacts and consequences will allow you to share the most convincing ones. The weights of each will vary according to the individual's style and the situation.

Here's how to *"flex "*your communication styles:

Direct: Select those that affect their accomplishments, freedom, prestige, authority, ability to influence, and opportunity for advancement.

Friendly: Select those that affect their reputation, freedom, fun on the job, and influential power. Testimonials and others' perceptions of their current behaviors will work best here.

Stable: Select those that affect their security, favorable environment, work patterns, and area of specialization. Others' perceptions will work well.

Analytical: Select those that affect their security, role, and ability to control their environment *(and you'd better be accurate!).*

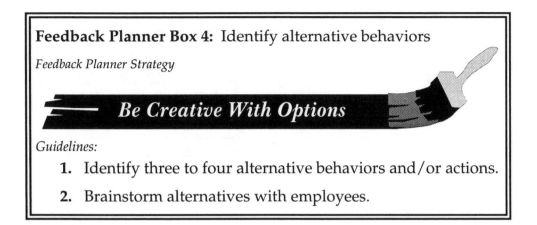

Feedback Planner Box 4: Identify alternative behaviors

Feedback Planner Strategy

Be Creative With Options

Guidelines:

1. Identify three to four alternative behaviors and/or actions.

2. Brainstorm alternatives with employees.

Here's how to *"flex"* your communication styles:

Direct and *Friendly:* Be ready for them to jump into solutions and action plans almost immediately. This is okay if you're sure they understand and accept Boxes 1, 2 and 3!

Stable and Analytical: Ask for their initial input, share a few of your own ideas, and prepare to break at this point. You can finish this feedback session later, after they've had a chance to collect their thoughts, questions and concerns.

Let's look at an application of *"flexing"* communication styles using the Feedback Planner.

Boss Matches Employee's Communication Style

Note: Notice here how Diane meets the needs, interests *and style* of her employee, Rick.

Diane prepares . . .
to give feedback to Rick, who has an **Analytical** style. Diane has a predominantly **Direct** style.

Diane knew she had to be *well-prepared* and *specific* when telling Rick *"why"* he should consider alternative behaviors. These are two keys to reaching an employee who has more of an **Analytical** communication style.

Diane's Feedback Planner:

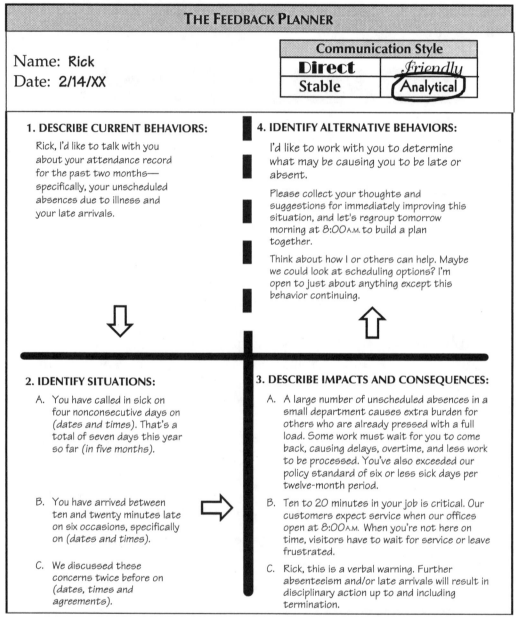

THE FEEDBACK PLANNER

Name: Rick
Date: 2/14/XX

Communication Style	
Direct	*friendly*
Stable	(Analytical)

1. DESCRIBE CURRENT BEHAVIORS:

Rick, I'd like to talk with you about your attendance record for the past two months—specifically, your unscheduled absences due to illness and your late arrivals.

4. IDENTIFY ALTERNATIVE BEHAVIORS:

I'd like to work with you to determine what may be causing you to be late or absent.

Please collect your thoughts and suggestions for immediately improving this situation, and let's regroup tomorrow morning at 8:00 A.M. to build a plan together.

Think about how I or others can help. Maybe we could look at scheduling options? I'm open to just about anything except this behavior continuing.

2. IDENTIFY SITUATIONS:

A. You have called in sick on four nonconsecutive days on (dates and times). That's a total of seven days this year so far (in five months).

B. You have arrived between ten and twenty minutes late on six occasions, specifically on (dates and times).

C. We discussed these concerns twice before on (dates, times and agreements).

3. DESCRIBE IMPACTS AND CONSEQUENCES:

A. A large number of unscheduled absences in a small department causes extra burden for others who are already pressed with a full load. Some work must wait for you to come back, causing delays, overtime, and less work to be processed. You've also exceeded our policy standard of six or less sick days per twelve-month period.

B. Ten to 20 minutes in your job is critical. Our customers expect service when our offices open at 8:00 A.M. When you're not here on time, visitors have to wait for service or leave frustrated.

C. Rick, this is a verbal warning. Further absenteeism and/or late arrivals will result in disciplinary action up to and including termination.

Alternative to avoid:

If Diane jumped directly into the conversation unprepared, she may have said exactly what she was thinking: *"Rick, I've had it with your cavalier attitude—coming in here when you choose (Box 1 Attacker). I've got a business to run with or without you. The way you're headed, it'll be without you. What's it gonna be? (Box 4 Abandoner and Pessimist)"*

Rick begins to analyze *"why"* he doesn't play the Lotto as much anymore.

LOTTO TICKET

Winner

1 2 3 4 5 6 7 8
9 10 11 12 13
14 15 16 17 18
19 20 21 22 23
24 25 26 27 28
29 30 31 32 33
34 35 36 37 38

Rick's Bag

Hawaii

Barbados

New York

CHAPTER NINE WORKSHEET: "STYLIZING" YOUR FEEDBACK

Apply the key learning points from Chapter Nine.

1. Use the *"Communication Styles"* tables in Chapter Nine as a reference for completing this *"flexing"* worksheet.

PERSON	GREATEST STYLE	GREATEST STRENGTH SHARING FEEDBACK WITH OTHERS	GREATEST WEAKNESS SHARING FEEDBACK WITH OTHERS	GREATEST PREFERENCE RECEIVING FEEDBACK FROM OTHERS
You:				
Your Boss:				
A Coworker:				
A Friend or Family Member:				
The Person You Will Give Feedback To Soon:				

2. Apply these key learning points to revise your Feedback Planner in Chapter Eight.

THE FEEDBACK PLANNER		
Name:	**Communication Style**	
	Direct	*Friendly*
Date:	Stable	Analytical

1. DESCRIBE CURRENT BEHAVIORS:

4. IDENTIFY ALTERNATIVE BEHAVIORS:

2. IDENTIFY SITUATIONS:

3. DESCRIBE IMPACTS AND CONSEQUENCES:

CHAPTER TEN

SUMMARY

The Feedback Planner provides a powerful formula—it gives you a way to improve your team's efforts and relationships by reinforcing commendable behavior with well-spoken praise. The tool provides a way to solve performance problems without the emotional heat that so often accompanies—and hinders—personnel encounters.

The Planner compels you to produce desired changes on the job using a new set of rules. The process helps you to equalize the playing field by treating others openly and professionally, regardless of hierarchical relationships. This ends offensive power plays and personal attacks.

The Feedback Planner leaves no room for subjective judgment. It opens channels of communication. It requires listening and respect from all parties.

People are complex resources. To keep workers focused and motivated, we can no longer bark complaints and threats, or *"toss out a bone once in a while to cheer up the troops."* Don't expect demoralized team members to continually come back for more.

We must be fair and equitable as we manage and build our most valuable assets. The Feedback Planner is a tool that will ensure employees not only come back for more—but give more, as well.

FEEDBACK PLANNER TEMPLATES

Use these Feedback Planner *"Templates"* to model and develop
Planners that directly fit your situations. Be aware that a few
points per box should suffice. Check and incorporate those
items from Boxes 3 and 4 that apply to your situation *(keep in
mind that these lists are not all-inclusive).*

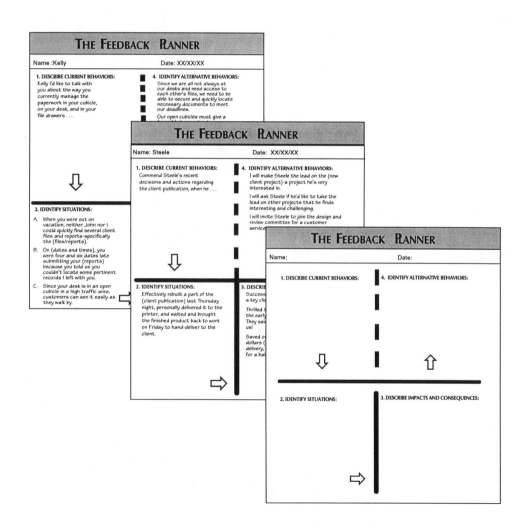

Any Behavior

Reference for your Feedback Planner:

THE FEEDBACK PLANNER

Name:	Date:

1. DESCRIBE CURRENT BEHAVIORS:

Focus on the employee's comments or a description of his behaviors—exactly what he said or did, or didn't say or do—nothing more.

Omit any judgmental or loaded words such as "bad," "rude," "insensitive," "unprofessional," "arrogant," etc.

4. IDENTIFY ALTERNATIVE BEHAVIORS:

Offer what can be done to improve the situation and to remove the undesirable impacts/consequences (listed below). What can you do, the employee do, the team do, etc.

Change the comments or behaviors, resources, training, time, environment, assignment, tools, goals, priorities, expectations, systems, policies, procedures, forms, perspectives, employment relationship, etc.

Gather more information.

Do nothing—it's always an option!

⇩   ⇧

2. IDENTIFY SITUATIONS:

Identify the specific times, places, and circumstances when the comments were heard or the behaviors were observed.

3. DESCRIBE IMPACTS AND CONSEQUENCES:

Focus on the impacts to the employee, you, team, company, customer, etc., short and long term effects, desirable and undesirable effects, etc. Filter with the receiver's communication style (see Chapter Nine for more ideas):

Direct: "Losses" of autonomy, authority, opportunities for input, leadership, etc.
Friendly: "Losses" of reputation, fun, social opportunities, influential power, etc. Testimonials and others' perceptions work well here.
Stable: "Losses" regarding security, teamwork, stability, favorable environment, balance, etc. Others' perceptions work well here.
Analytical: "Losses" of role, clarity, accuracy, information, ability to control environment, etc.

Other losses include:
Low morale, productivity, business, credibility, reputation, confidence, etc.
More work, rework, pressure, delays, expenses, and losses.
Poor use of resources, inefficiencies, and breakdowns.
Offended workers, complaining customers, management, legal action, etc.
Discipline or obstructions to advancement.
Life-threatening burnout, ulcers, heart attacks.

⇨

1. Inappropriate

"Shane, we will not tolerate that kind of look around here. Change your looks or change your job!"

1. Appropriate

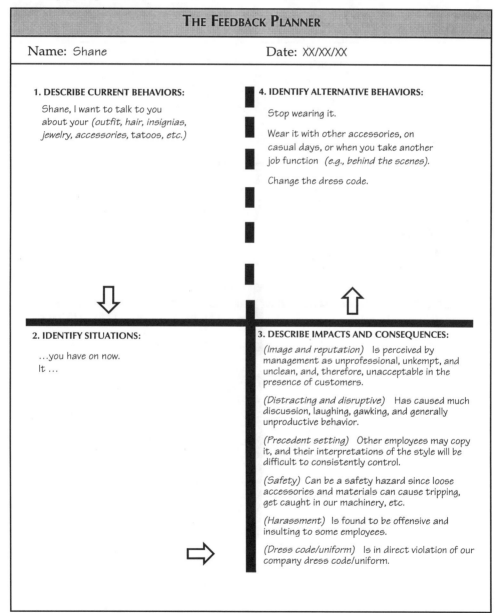

THE FEEDBACK PLANNER

Name: Shane   **Date:** XX/XX/XX

1. DESCRIBE CURRENT BEHAVIORS:

Shane, I want to talk to you about your *(outfit, hair, insignias, jewelry, accessories, tatoos, etc.)*

4. IDENTIFY ALTERNATIVE BEHAVIORS:

Stop wearing it.

Wear it with other accessories, on casual days, or when you take another job function *(e.g., behind the scenes).*

Change the dress code.

2. IDENTIFY SITUATIONS:

…you have on now.
It …

3. DESCRIBE IMPACTS AND CONSEQUENCES:

(Image and reputation) Is perceived by management as unprofessional, unkempt, and unclean, and, therefore, unacceptable in the presence of customers.

(Distracting and disruptive) Has caused much discussion, laughing, gawking, and generally unproductive behavior.

(Precedent setting) Other employees may copy it, and their interpretations of the style will be difficult to consistently control.

(Safety) Can be a safety hazard since loose accessories and materials can cause tripping, get caught in our machinery, etc.

(Harassment) Is found to be offensive and insulting to some employees.

(Dress code/uniform) Is in direct violation of our company dress code/uniform.

2. Inappropriate

"Bart, I'm sorry to tell you this, but you smell. Do you take baths daily?"

2. Appropriate

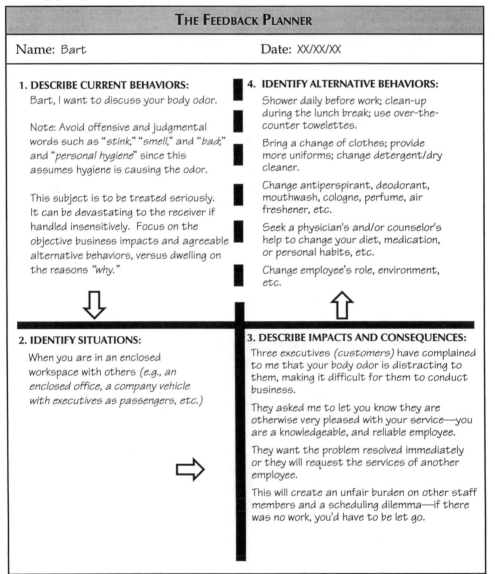

THE FEEDBACK PLANNER	
Name: Bart	Date: XX/XX/XX

1. DESCRIBE CURRENT BEHAVIORS:

Bart, I want to discuss your body odor.

Note: Avoid offensive and judgmental words such as *"stink," "smell,"* and *"bad;"* and *"personal hygiene"* since this assumes hygiene is causing the odor.

This subject is to be treated seriously. It can be devastating to the receiver if handled insensitively. Focus on the objective business impacts and agreeable alternative behaviors, versus dwelling on the reasons *"why."*

4. IDENTIFY ALTERNATIVE BEHAVIORS:

Shower daily before work; clean-up during the lunch break; use over-the-counter towelettes.

Bring a change of clothes; provide more uniforms; change detergent/dry cleaner.

Change antiperspirant, deodorant, mouthwash, cologne, perfume, air freshener, etc.

Seek a physician's and/or counselor's help to change your diet, medication, or personal habits, etc.

Change employee's role, environment, etc.

2. IDENTIFY SITUATIONS:

When you are in an enclosed workspace with others (e.g., an enclosed office, a company vehicle with executives as passengers, etc.)

3. DESCRIBE IMPACTS AND CONSEQUENCES:

Three executives (customers) have complained to me that your body odor is distracting to them, making it difficult for them to conduct business.

They asked me to let you know they are otherwise very pleased with your service—you are a knowledgeable, and reliable employee.

They want the problem resolved immediately or they will request the services of another employee.

This will create an unfair burden on other staff members and a scheduling dilemma—if there was no work, you'd have to be let go.

3. Inappropriate

"Bill, I don't know what's been going on outside of work—it's none of my business. But your attitude has really been poor lately. It seems like you don't care about your role on our team anymore. You're constantly missing meetings, and some of us are starting to avoid you. You really need to get your act together."

3. Appropriate

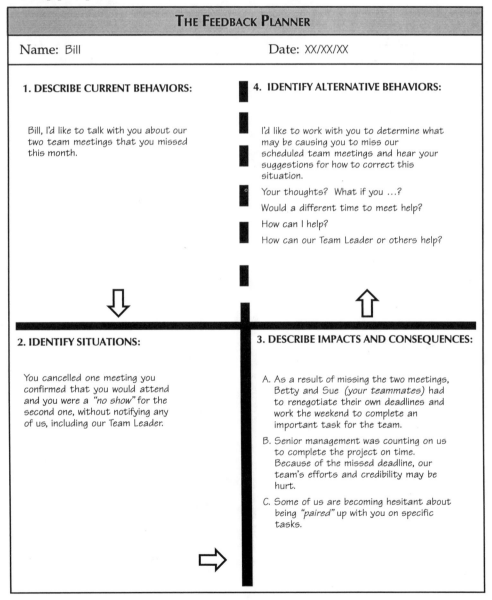

THE FEEDBACK PLANNER

Name: Bill   Date: XX/XX/XX

1. DESCRIBE CURRENT BEHAVIORS:

Bill, I'd like to talk with you about our two team meetings that you missed this month.

4. IDENTIFY ALTERNATIVE BEHAVIORS:

I'd like to work with you to determine what may be causing you to miss our scheduled team meetings and hear your suggestions for how to correct this situation.

Your thoughts? What if you …?

Would a different time to meet help?

How can I help?

How can our Team Leader or others help?

2. IDENTIFY SITUATIONS:

You cancelled one meeting you confirmed that you would attend and you were a *"no show"* for the second one, without notifying any of us, including our Team Leader.

3. DESCRIBE IMPACTS AND CONSEQUENCES:

A. As a result of missing the two meetings, Betty and Sue *(your teammates)* had to renegotiate their own deadlines and work the weekend to complete an important task for the team.

B. Senior management was counting on us to complete the project on time. Because of the missed deadline, our team's efforts and credibility may be hurt.

C. Some of us are becoming hesitant about being *"paired"* up with you on specific tasks.

4. Inappropriate

"Tran, I'm sorry to tell you this, but your presentations can be boring, or so I've heard. Maybe you should look into attending a training class or something?"

4. Appropriate

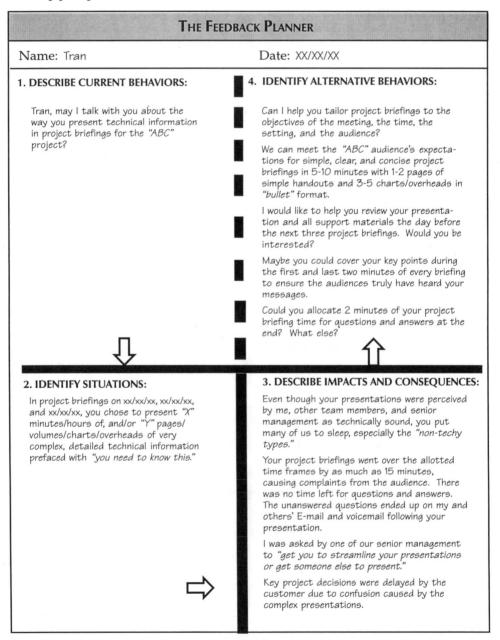

THE FEEDBACK PLANNER	
Name: Tran	**Date:** XX/XX/XX

1. DESCRIBE CURRENT BEHAVIORS:

Tran, may I talk with you about the way you present technical information in project briefings for the "ABC" project?

4. IDENTIFY ALTERNATIVE BEHAVIORS:

Can I help you tailor project briefings to the objectives of the meeting, the time, the setting, and the audience?

We can meet the "ABC" audience's expectations for simple, clear, and concise project briefings in 5-10 minutes with 1-2 pages of simple handouts and 3-5 charts/overheads in "bullet" format.

I would like to help you review your presentation and all support materials the day before the next three project briefings. Would you be interested?

Maybe you could cover your key points during the first and last two minutes of every briefing to ensure the audiences truly have heard your messages.

Could you allocate 2 minutes of your project briefing time for questions and answers at the end? What else?

2. IDENTIFY SITUATIONS:

In project briefings on xx/xx/xx, xx/xx/xx, and xx/xx/xx, you chose to present "X" minutes/hours of, and/or "Y" pages/volumes/charts/overheads of very complex, detailed technical information prefaced with "you need to know this."

3. DESCRIBE IMPACTS AND CONSEQUENCES:

Even though your presentations were perceived by me, other team members, and senior management as technically sound, you put many of us to sleep, especially the "non-techy types."

Your project briefings went over the allotted time frames by as much as 15 minutes, causing complaints from the audience. There was no time left for questions and answers. The unanswered questions ended up on my and others' E-mail and voicemail following your presentation.

I was asked by one of our senior management to "get you to streamline your presentations or get someone else to present."

Key project decisions were delayed by the customer due to confusion caused by the complex presentations.

5. Inappropriate

"Juan, you've been walking on thin ice lately by being careless with your comments and work that you give directly to customers and senior management. Now I question whether you're right for the job ..."

5. Appropriate

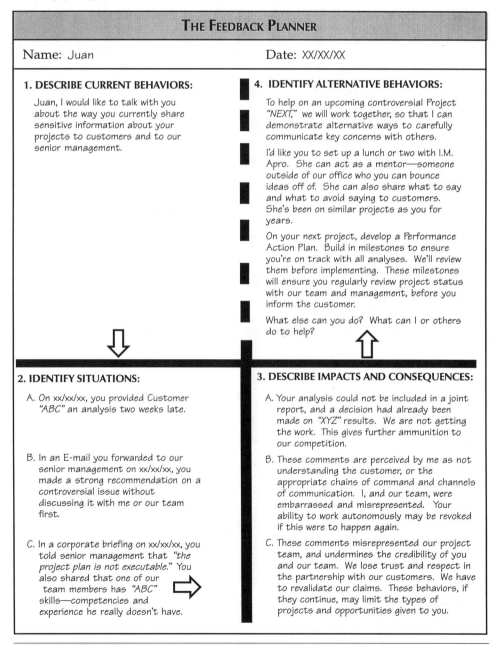

THE FEEDBACK PLANNER

Name: Juan   Date: XX/XX/XX

1. DESCRIBE CURRENT BEHAVIORS:

Juan, I would like to talk with you about the way you currently share sensitive information about your projects to customers and to our senior management.

4. IDENTIFY ALTERNATIVE BEHAVIORS:

To help on an upcoming controversial Project "NEXT," we will work together, so that I can demonstrate alternative ways to carefully communicate key concerns with others.

I'd like you to set up a lunch or two with I.M. Apro. She can act as a mentor—someone outside of our office who you can bounce ideas off of. She can also share what to say and what to avoid saying to customers. She's been on similar projects as you for years.

On your next project, develop a Performance Action Plan. Build in milestones to ensure you're on track with all analyses. We'll review them before implementing. These milestones will ensure you regularly review project status with our team and management, before you inform the customer.

What else can you do? What can I or others do to help?

2. IDENTIFY SITUATIONS:

A. On xx/xx/xx, you provided Customer "ABC" an analysis two weeks late.

B. In an E-mail you forwarded to our senior management on xx/xx/xx, you made a strong recommendation on a controversial issue without discussing it with me or our team first.

C. In a corporate briefing on xx/xx/xx, you told senior management that *"the project plan is not executable."* You also shared that one of our team members has *"ABC"* skills—competencies and experience he really doesn't have.

3. DESCRIBE IMPACTS AND CONSEQUENCES:

A. Your analysis could not be included in a joint report, and a decision had already been made on "XYZ" results. We are not getting the work. This gives further ammunition to our competition.

B. These comments are perceived by me as not understanding the customer, or the appropriate chains of command and channels of communication. I, and our team, were embarrassed and misrepresented. Your ability to work autonomously may be revoked if this were to happen again.

C. These comments misrepresented our project team, and undermines the credibility of you and our team. We lose trust and respect in the partnership with our customers. We have to revalidate our claims. These behaviors, if they continue, may limit the types of projects and opportunities given to you.

6. Inappropriate

"Kevin, I know you're the boss, but I'm having problems with Hank. He's just not doing his part on Project 'ABC.' I'm not sure he has the skills. Anyway, it's not my business to reprimand my peers—I'll leave it up to you ..."

6. Appropriate

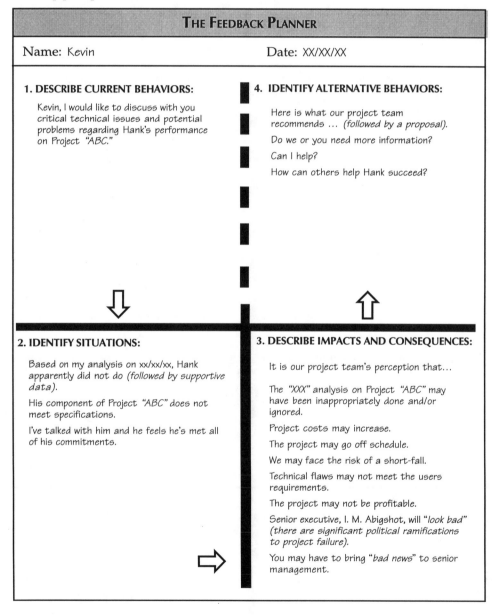

THE FEEDBACK PLANNER	
Name: Kevin	**Date:** XX/XX/XX

1. DESCRIBE CURRENT BEHAVIORS:

Kevin, I would like to discuss with you critical technical issues and potential problems regarding Hank's performance on Project "ABC."

4. IDENTIFY ALTERNATIVE BEHAVIORS:

Here is what our project team recommends ... *(followed by a proposal).*

Do we or you need more information?

Can I help?

How can others help Hank succeed?

2. IDENTIFY SITUATIONS:

Based on my analysis on xx/xx/xx, Hank apparently did not do *(followed by supportive data).*

His component of Project "ABC" does not meet specifications.

I've talked with him and he feels he's met all of his commitments.

3. DESCRIBE IMPACTS AND CONSEQUENCES:

It is our project team's perception that...

The "XXX" analysis on Project "ABC" may have been inappropriately done and/or ignored.

Project costs may increase.

The project may go off schedule.

We may face the risk of a short-fall.

Technical flaws may not meet the users requirements.

The project may not be profitable.

Senior executive, I. M. Abigshot, will *"look bad"* *(there are significant political ramifications to project failure).*

You may have to bring *"bad news"* to senior management.

7. Inappropriate

"Bonnie, you're definitely my best hire so far. I'm really happy with how you take charge and get things done. You'll be going places around here!"

7. Appropriate

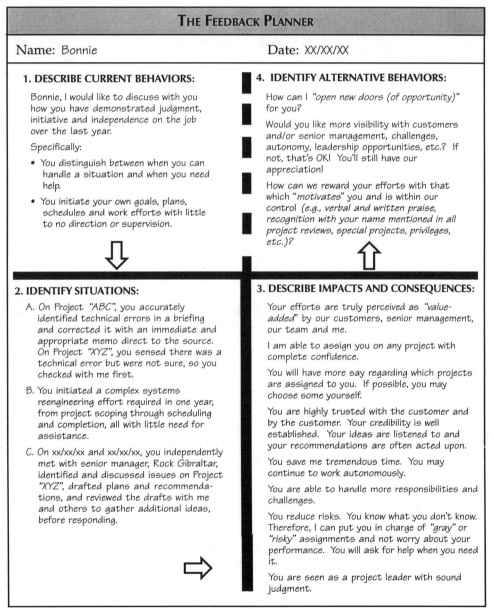

THE FEEDBACK PLANNER	
Name: Bonnie	Date: XX/XX/XX

1. DESCRIBE CURRENT BEHAVIORS:

Bonnie, I would like to discuss with you how you have demonstrated judgment, initiative and independence on the job over the last year.

Specifically:

- You distinguish between when you can handle a situation and when you need help.
- You initiate your own goals, plans, schedules and work efforts with little to no direction or supervision.

4. IDENTIFY ALTERNATIVE BEHAVIORS:

How can I *"open new doors (of opportunity)"* for you?

Would you like more visibility with customers and/or senior management, challenges, autonomy, leadership opportunities, etc.? If not, that's OK! You'll still have our appreciation!

How can we reward your efforts with that which *"motivates"* you and is within our control (*e.g., verbal and written praise, recognition with your name mentioned in all project reviews, special projects, privileges, etc.*)?

2. IDENTIFY SITUATIONS:

A. On Project *"ABC"*, you accurately identified technical errors in a briefing and corrected it with an immediate and appropriate memo direct to the source. On Project *"XYZ"*, you sensed there was a technical error but were not sure, so you checked with me first.

B. You initiated a complex systems reengineering effort required in one year, from project scoping through scheduling and completion, all with little need for assistance.

C. On xx/xx/xx and xx/xx/xx, you independently met with senior manager, Rock Gibraltar, identified and discussed issues on Project *"XYZ"*, drafted plans and recommendations, and reviewed the drafts with me and others to gather additional ideas, before responding.

3. DESCRIBE IMPACTS AND CONSEQUENCES:

Your efforts are truly perceived as *"value-added"* by our customers, senior management, our team and me.

I am able to assign you on any project with complete confidence.

You will have more say regarding which projects are assigned to you. If possible, you may choose some yourself.

You are highly trusted with the customer and by the customer. Your credibility is well established. Your ideas are listened to and your recommendations are often acted upon.

You save me tremendous time. You may continue to work autonomously.

You are able to handle more responsibilities and challenges.

You reduce risks. You know what you don't know. Therefore, I can put you in charge of *"gray"* or *"risky"* assignments and not worry about your performance. You will ask for help when you need it.

You are seen as a project leader with sound judgment.

8. Inappropriate

"Curt, what's with you lately?! You've been a 'Lone Ranger,' cutting all of us out of the picture. We're all looking like idiots on this project. Now will you please start including us in your thoughts and actions?!"

8. Appropriate

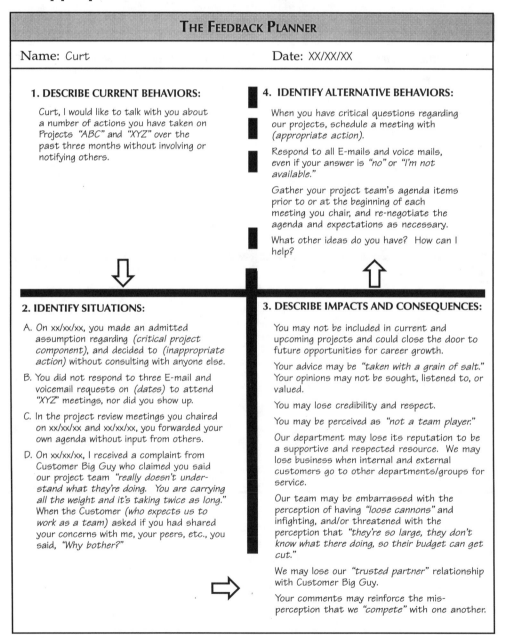

THE FEEDBACK PLANNER	
Name: Curt	Date: XX/XX/XX

1. DESCRIBE CURRENT BEHAVIORS:

Curt, I would like to talk with you about a number of actions you have taken on Projects "ABC" and "XYZ" over the past three months without involving or notifying others.

4. IDENTIFY ALTERNATIVE BEHAVIORS:

When you have critical questions regarding our projects, schedule a meeting with *(appropriate action)*.

Respond to all E-mails and voice mails, even if your answer is *"no"* or *"I'm not available."*

Gather your project team's agenda items prior to or at the beginning of each meeting you chair, and re-negotiate the agenda and expectations as necessary.

What other ideas do you have? How can I help?

2. IDENTIFY SITUATIONS:

A. On xx/xx/xx, you made an admitted assumption regarding *(critical project component)*, and decided to *(inappropriate action)* without consulting with anyone else.

B. You did not respond to three E-mail and voicemail requests on *(dates)* to attend "XYZ" meetings, nor did you show up.

C. In the project review meetings you chaired on xx/xx/xx and xx/xx/xx, you forwarded your own agenda without input from others.

D. On xx/xx/xx, I received a complaint from Customer Big Guy who claimed you said our project team *"really doesn't under-stand what they're doing. You are carrying all the weight and it's taking twice as long."* When the Customer *(who expects us to work as a team)* asked if you had shared your concerns with me, your peers, etc., you said, *"Why bother?"*

3. DESCRIBE IMPACTS AND CONSEQUENCES:

You may not be included in current and upcoming projects and could close the door to future opportunities for career growth.

Your advice may be *"taken with a grain of salt."* Your opinions may not be sought, listened to, or valued.

You may lose credibility and respect.

You may be perceived as *"not a team player."*

Our department may lose its reputation to be a supportive and respected resource. We may lose business when internal and external customers go to other departments/groups for service.

Our team may be embarrassed with the perception of having *"loose cannons"* and infighting, and/or threatened with the perception that *"they're so large, they don't know what there doing, so their budget can get cut."*

We may lose our *"trusted partner"* relationship with Customer Big Guy.

Your comments may reinforce the mis-perception that we *"compete"* with one another.

REPRODUCIBLE FORMS

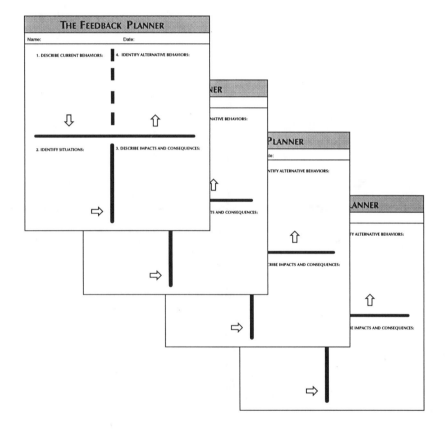

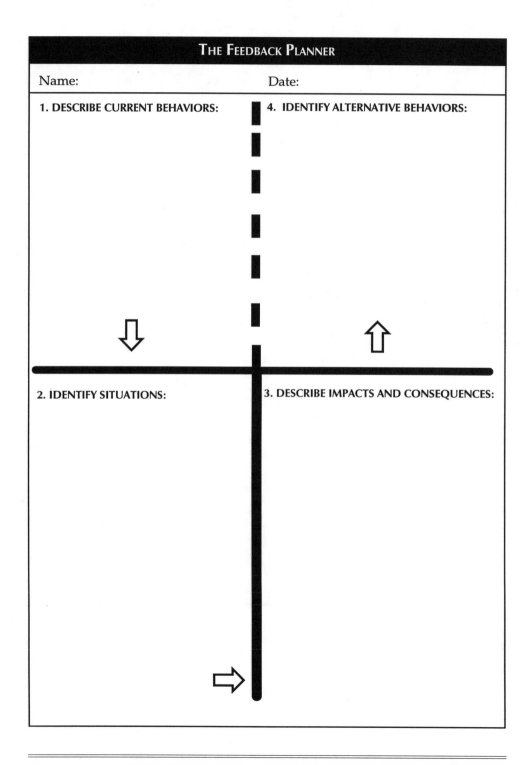

THE FEEDBACK PLANNER

Name: Date:

1. DESCRIBE CURRENT BEHAVIORS: **4. IDENTIFY ALTERNATIVE BEHAVIORS:**

2. IDENTIFY SITUATIONS: **3. DESCRIBE IMPACTS AND CONSEQUENCES:**

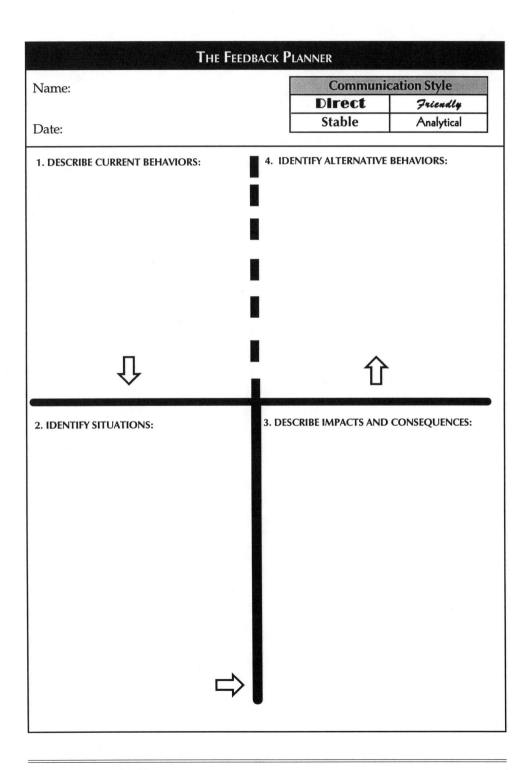

THE FEEDBACK PLANNER		

Name:

Date:

Communication Style	
Direct	*Friendly*
Stable	Analytical

1. DESCRIBE CURRENT BEHAVIORS:

4. IDENTIFY ALTERNATIVE BEHAVIORS:

2. IDENTIFY SITUATIONS:

3. DESCRIBE IMPACTS AND CONSEQUENCES:

PROFESSIONAL AND PERSONAL DEVELOPMENT PUBLICATIONS FROM RICHARD CHANG ASSOCIATES, INC.

Designed to support continuous learning, these highly targeted, integrated collections from Richard Chang Associates, Inc. (RCA) help individuals and organizations acquire the knowledge and skills needed to succeed in today's ever-changing workplace. Titles are available through RCA, Jossey-Bass, Inc., fine bookstores, and distributors internationally.

PRACTICAL GUIDEBOOK COLLECTION

QUALITY IMPROVEMENT SERIES

Continuous Process Improvement
Continuous Improvement Tools, Volume 1
Continuous Improvement Tools, Volume 2
Step-By-Step Problem Solving
Meetings That Work!
Improving Through Benchmarking
Succeeding As A Self-Managed Team
Measuring Organizational Improvement Impact
Process Reengineering In Action
Satisfying Internal Customers First!

MANAGEMENT SKILLS SERIES

Interviewing And Selecting High Performers
On-The-Job Orientation And Training
Coaching Through Effective Feedback
Expanding Leadership Impact
Mastering Change Management
Re-Creating Teams During Transitions
Planning Successful Employee Performance
Coaching For Peak Employee Performance
Evaluating Employee Performance

HIGH PERFORMANCE TEAM SERIES

Success Through Teamwork
Building A Dynamic Team
Measuring Team Performance
Team Decision-Making Techniques

HIGH-IMPACT TRAINING SERIES

Creating High-Impact Training
Identifying Targeted Training Needs
Mapping A Winning Training Approach
Producing High-Impact Learning Tools
Applying Successful Training Techniques
Measuring The Impact Of Training
Make Your Training Results Last

WORKPLACE DIVERSITY SERIES

Capitalizing On Workplace Diversity
Successful Staffing In A Diverse Workplace
Team Building For Diverse Work Groups
Communicating In A Diverse Workplace
Tools For Valuing Diversity

PERSONAL GROWTH AND DEVELOPMENT COLLECTION

Managing Your Career in a Changing Workplace
Unlocking Your Career Potential
Marketing Yourself and Your Career
Making Career Transitions
Memory Tips For The Forgetful

101 STUPID THINGS COLLECTION

101 Stupid Things Trainers Do To Sabotage Success
101 Stupid Things Supervisors Do To Sabotage Success
101 Stupid Things Employees Do To Sabotage Success
101 Stupid Things Salespeople Do To Sabotage Success
101 Stupid Things Business Travelers Do To Sabotage Success

ABOUT RICHARD CHANG ASSOCIATES, INC.

Richard Chang Associates, Inc. (RCA) is a multi-disciplinary organizational performance improvement firm. Since 1987, RCA has provided private and public sector clients around the world with the experience, expertise, and resources needed to build capability in such critical areas as process improvement, management development, project management, team performance, performance measurement, and facilitator training. RCA's comprehensive package of services, products, and publications reflect the firm's commitment to practical, innovative approaches and to the achievement of significant, measurable results.

RCA RESOURCES OPTIMIZE ORGANIZATIONAL PERFORMANCE

CONSULTING — Using a broad range of skills, knowledge, and tools, RCA consultants assist clients in developing and implementing a wide range of performance improvement initiatives.

TRAINING — Practical, "real world" training programs are designed with a "take initiative" emphasis. Options include off-the-shelf programs, customized programs, and public and on-site seminars.

CURRICULUM AND MATERIALS DEVELOPMENT — A cost-effective and flexible alternative to internal staffing, RCA can custom-develop and/or customize content to meet both organizational objectives and specific program needs.

VIDEO PRODUCTION — RCA's award-winning, custom video productions provide employees with information in a consistent manner that achieves lasting impact.

PUBLICATIONS — The comprehensive and practical collection of publications from RCA supports organizational training initiatives and self-directed learning.

PACKAGED PROGRAMS — Designed for first-time and experienced trainers alike, these programs offer comprehensive, integrated materials (including selected Practical Guidebooks) that provide a wide range of flexible training options. Choose from:

- Meetings That Work! ToolPAK™
- Step-By-Step Problem Solving ToolKIT™
- Continuous Process Improvement Packaged Training Program
- Continuous Improvement Tools, Volume 1 ToolPAK™
- Continuous Improvement Tools, Volume 2 ToolPAK™
- High Involvement Teamwork™ Packaged Training Program

RICHARD
CHANG
ASSOCIATES

World Class Resources. World Class Results.[SM]

Richard Chang Associates, Inc.
Corporate Headquarters
15265 Alton Parkway, Suite 300, Irvine, California 92618 USA
(800) 756-8096 • (949) 727-7477 • Fax: (949) 727-7007
E-Mail: info@rca4results.com • www.richardchangassociates.com

U.S. Offices in Irvine and Atlanta • Licensees and Distributors Worldwide